PLAYING OUT OF BOUNDS

"Belonging" and the North American Chinese Invitational Volleyball Tournament

Playing Out of Bounds investigates the North American Chinese Invitational Volleyball Tournament (NACIVT), an annual event that began in the 1930s in the streets of Manhattan and now attracts over 1,200 competitors from the United States and Canada. Its two key features are the nine-man game, where there are nine instead of the usual six volleyball players on the court, and the fact that player eligibility is limited to "100 per cent Chinese" and Asian players, as defined in the tournament rules. The league justifies this eligibility rule based on the racism that early Chinese Americans faced when they were denied access to physical activity spaces, and on the discrimination that continues to limit Asian people's opportunities both in and outside of sport.

Drawing on interviews, participant-observation, and analysis of websites and tournament documents, *Playing Out of Bounds* explores how participants understand and negotiate their sense of belonging within the NACIVT's community of volleyball players and how the boundaries of this community are continually being (re)defined. This identity- and community-building occurs within a context of anti-Asian racism, growing numbers of mixed-race players, and fluidity of what it means to be Canadian, American, Chinese, and Asian.

YUKA NAKAMURA is an associate professor in the School of Kinesiology and Health Science at York University.

T0339212

PLAYING OUT OF BOUNDS

"Belonging" and the North American Chinese Invitational Volleyball Tournament

Yuka Nakamura

UNIVERSITY OF TORONTO PRESS
Toronto Buffalo London

© University of Toronto Press 2019
Toronto Buffalo London
utorontopress.com

ISBN 978-1-4875-0499-1 (cloth)   ISBN 978-1-4875-2364-0 (paper)

Library and Archives Canada Cataloguing in Publication

Title: Playing out of bounds : "belonging" and the North American Chinese
  Invitational Volleyball Tournament / Yuka Nakamura.
Names: Nakamura, Yuka, 1976–, author.
Description: Includes bibliographical references and index.
Identifiers: Canadiana 20190103345 | ISBN 9781487523640 (paper) |
  ISBN 9781487504991 (cloth)
Subjects: LCSH: North American Chinese Invitational Volleyball
  Tournament. | LCSH: Volleyball – Tournaments – Social aspects – United
  States. | LCSH: Volleyball – Tournaments – Social aspects – Canada. |
  LCSH: Chinese Americans – Ethnic identity. | LCSH: Belonging
  (Social psychology) | CSH: Chinese Canadians – Ethnic identity.
Classification: LCC GV1015.55 .N35 2019 | DDC 796.325089/951073 – dc23

University of Toronto Press acknowledges the financial assistance to its
publishing program of the Canada Council for the Arts and the Ontario Arts
Council, an agency of the Government of Ontario.

 Canada Council   Conseil des Arts
for the Arts   du Canada

 ONTARIO ARTS COUNCIL
CONSEIL DES ARTS DE L'ONTARIO
an Ontario government agency
un organisme du gouvernement de l'Ontario

Funded by the   Financé par le
Government   gouvernement
of Canada   du Canada
 Canadä

Contents

Acknowledgments

I am indebted to the participants of the North American Chinese Invitational Volleyball Tournament (NACIVT) and to those who shared themselves and their experiences with me. It is my hope that I have honoured their stories, the complexities of their lives, and the multiple meanings of their involvement in the NACIVT.

I am also grateful to those who allowed me to include their photos and likenesses in this book, so that the tournament could come to life in these pages. Thank you also to Walter Low and Rosanna U for sharing their photos and for their assistance in contacting players.

I must also thank members of my intellectual community who inspired, challenged, and supported me in the very early stages of this book. I wish I could name them all. Let me just say thank you to the "Sussex Gang" and to Peter Donnelly, my teacher and mentor. I also wish to acknowledge my colleagues and friends at York University, particularly Parissa Safai, Hernán Humaña, and Lyndsay Hayhurst, who have been enthusiastic supporters of my work generally and of this book specifically.

I would also like to express my gratitude to the anonymous reviewers who patiently read revision after revision and provided invaluable feedback and suggestions. I am thankful for your time and your generosity in sharing your insights.

This book would also not have been possible without the support of the University of Toronto Press, especially Jodi Lewchuk and the members of the Manuscript Review Committee, copy-editor

Margaret Allen, and associate managing editor Janice Evans and the rest of the in-house editorial staff. Thank you for guiding this book to this point. I am also indebted to Douglas Hildebrand for his patience, which showed no limits. I am grateful to Canadian Scholars' Press for allowing me to reprint parts of "Playing in Chinatown: A Critical Discussion of the Nation/Sport/Citizen Triad," from *Race and Sport in Canada: Intersecting Inequalities* (2012). In addition, I would like to thank the York Centre for Asian Research for their assistance through the YCAR Publication Support Fund.

A special thank you to Rosanne Aleong and to my "JLC," Mia Kim, Maggie Kishibe, and Jennifer Maeba; your friendship has never wavered during this journey and beyond. I am also grateful for the encouragement of my family: Ben; Bhavana and Mahendra Shah; and Sheetal, Ramu, Neil, and Maya Shenoy.

There are no words to express my gratitude to my husband, Nirtal Shah. Nirtal is my partner, my safe harbour, and my champion in all that I do. He inspires me to challenge myself, to be brave, and to move "on to the next." I am thankful for his infinite patience, wisdom, and guidance throughout this project and every endeavour, big or small, that I have undertaken. I am so blessed to have a partner who sees me for who I am and who can also see so much possibility, even when I can't.

My children, Ayumi and Akash, are my greatest joy. They remind me not to take life so seriously, to play, to sing, to be silly, and to have dance parties. The simplicity of the things that give them pleasure – a good joke, a book, a playdate – brings into sharp relief what truly matters. They both amaze me with their courage, their capacity to forgive, and their acceptance. I have so much to learn from them.

Finally, I would like to thank my parents. Kumiko and Tatsushi Nakamura, and my brother, Aki Nakamura. Much of how my intellectual journey has taken shape is intertwined with your migration from Japan. I dedicate this book to you in honour of your courage and the lives you have made for yourselves in Canada.

PLAYING OUT OF BOUNDS

"Belonging" and the North American Chinese Invitational Volleyball Tournament

Chapter 1

Introduction

Washington, DC, was in the midst of another heat wave on day one of the annual North American Chinese Invitational Volleyball Tournament (NACIVT). It was only 8:00 a.m., but the air was already thick with humidity. From arranging the tournament space, sweeping away debris, laying out the lines of the court, or setting up the nets, the men and women were already dewy with sweat. As the day wore on, the heat and the sun became unbearable, even for me, a bystander. There were very few if any trees in the parking lot where the tournament was taking place. Players had brought tents and canopies to store coolers filled with ice, water, and sports drinks and to rest in the shade between bouts. I had opened up my umbrella, as many of the other observers – and even the referees – had done, to keep the sun off. Even with my umbrella, sunglasses, and hat, I felt the heat coming off the concrete where close to 100 volleyball teams were competing. Certainly, the tournament could have taken place indoors in a comfortable, air-conditioned setting where there was no heat, glare, wind, humidity, or sudden rain shower with which to contend. Instead, the men and women played on unforgiving concrete that damaged their knees and backs with every block and every dig and left them picking gravel and stones out of their skin.

Even after three and a half hours of playing in such conditions, the participants' intensity had not waned. Their skin shone with a mixture of sweat and sunscreen, and players frequently pulled up their shirts and sleeves to wipe their faces. The players blocked and spiked with ferocity, and dove without heeding the concrete under them, to keep a ball in play. They yelled to claim a ball, celebrate a point, or express frustration. Those on the sidelines – teammates or club mates, friends, parents, and partners – cheered their teams on with equal fervour.

By the time a game ended, the players were covered with a fine layer of the dirt and dust coming off the ground. Some of them were still elated from a win, grinning, locking arms with one another, and exchanging high-fives. Others looked more serious, fatigued, or disappointed. After or between bouts, players often socialized with their teammates or with players from other teams. But as the day progressed and the heat and fatigue intensified, each tent grew quieter. Some players continued to socialize with other competitors or watch other teams, even after their team's last game of the day. In contrast, other players nursed an injury with ice packs on their knees and ankles, replaced the tape on their fingers and other parts of their bodies, or lay on towels and grass cloth mats with their arms flung over their eyes. This was the event that they had been working towards since spring. This was the climax of their summer: to compete in the North American Chinese Invitational Volleyball Tournament.

Having never personally been a part of a sports team that competed with the kind of intensity that I witnessed at the tournaments, nor having played sports under the types of conditions that the players encountered during the three-day annual tournament, I had a hard time understanding what motivated these individuals to play in this multi-day tournament, in punishing heat, with a high risk of injury. Surely there were other opportunities to play volleyball in the comfort of an air-conditioned space? Even beach volleyball would be easier on the joints. Further still, many players had been participating for years, travelling from city to city, and paying to play in a tournament that had only bragging rights and no monetary prize. While playing volleyball was obviously critical to the experience, the participants also enjoyed the relationships and friendships fostered through their involvement. Why else, following hours of gruelling competition and circumstances, would they stay after their scheduled matches to watch or support other

teams? Or even after returning to their hotel rooms, what com-
pelled them to go back out to a local bar or dance club and socialize
with teammates and rivals rather than crawl into bed and rest their
weary bodies in preparation for the next day of competition? Even
more intriguing for me was how individuals like Karen,[1] who felt
that the racialized eligibility rules made the NACIVT "a racist volleyball league," nevertheless participated for years, six in her case.

Indeed, it was Karen who first introduced me to the NACIVT.
I had been interviewing her for another research project on the
growing diversity of post-secondary physical education programs,
and it was these words, "Oh, yeah … I play in a racist volleyball
league," and their casual delivery that immediately piqued my
interest in the tournament. When she explained that there were eligibility rules that would permit me, a person of Japanese descent
to play, but also limit my playing time because I was not Chinese,
I immediately felt this was unfair and briefly saw myself exposing
this injustice. Now that I have spoken to numerous participants
and attended several tournaments, it is no longer so easy for me
to take this position. There was more to the eligibility rules than
exclusion.

In fact, the more I spoke with Karen and other NACIVT participants, the more intrigued and puzzled I became by the fact that
she and others could describe teammates and the friends made
through the tournament as family, even when these same individuals did not help to redress the unfairness of the eligibility
rules or, in some instances, benefited from or even endorsed them.
What drew individuals who are subjected to racism and discrimination because of racialized notions of eligibility and therefore
membership to participate? How could they simultaneously feel a
sense of belonging while being marginalized within the NACIVT
community?

Identity, belonging, and how they are understood in relation to
socially constructed notions of race, gender, and culture are interro-
gated through this study of the North American Chinese Invitational

---

1 All names are pseudonyms. Team and club names in some instances have also been
changed to ensure anonymity.

Volleyball Tournament. Specifically, I identify the contours and context of the community that participation in the NACIVT produces. I examine the processes through which a collective "we" is produced in relation to difference, and how ideas of race, gender, and culture are mobilized and deployed in these processes. This project is therefore grounded in the assumption that this collective "we" or "community" is not stable. Rather, I demonstrate the ways in which community is stabilized and made to seem homogeneous and unified through the continual naming, policing, redefining, and resisting of boundaries of belonging and membership that occur in and through the NACIVT. In examining how boundaries, defined along racial lines, are contested within the NACIVT, we can better understand the racialization and social construction of diaspora. Namely, this book illustrates how home and feeling at home are negotiated constructs that involve ongoing processes of seeking and granting membership, and of including and prohibiting, processes that occur along various lines of exclusion.

This project addresses gaps in the scholarship on Asians in Canada and the United States in the sociology of sport and physical culture, and on sport in Asian diaspora studies; however, there are other equally important reasons for this research. Although the tournament has been successfully organized for several decades and has grown in popularity each year, there is little published information, in scholarship or in archives, about the event, its history, or the experiences of participants. In addition, there are fewer and fewer individuals who participated in and remember the early tournaments. Though a scholarly contribution is essential, equally important are the memories and experiences of the participants. Such stories help to destabilize the myth of Asian frailty and lack of interest in sporting activities.

This book is based on a multi-sited ethnography where I interviewed participants, observed tournaments, and analysed texts such as websites and tournament-related documents (see the appendix). The primary method used was semi-structured, in-depth interviews with individuals recruited through my existing contacts, snowball, and purposeful sampling. Interviews were primarily conducted in person, though a few were done via email or by telephone. Most of the interviews took place between 2005 and 2007. In 2015,

I conducted an additional eight interviews to identify any changes in and the salience of the original themes. Many of these subsequent interviews took place in Toronto, Canada. In total, I interviewed 41 individuals. While every attempt was made to include diverse experiences, the interviewees tended to identify as male (22 male players; 19 female players) and as Chinese (32 Chinese players, 4 "half-Chinese" players, and 5 "non-Chinese" players). The ages ranged from 19 to 66 at the time of the interviews, with most interviewees being in their twenties and thirties. They also varied in their generational context, though most participants were second-generation immigrants. Coaches (14), players (41), alumni (12), organizers (8), captains (4), and elders (3) were represented in this group. All of the players were well educated, pursuing or having earned one or more post-secondary degrees. Six interviewees were students, while others worked in finance, entertainment, sales and marketing, education, technology, and the civil service or were self-employed. In total, individuals from eleven different teams that were linked to six cities – Washington, Toronto, Boston, New York, Montreal, and San Francisco – were involved in this study (see table 1.1 for more information about the interviewees).

I also observed four tournaments to supplement the interview data. Specifically, I attended two annual tournaments or "Majors," the first in Toronto, Ontario, from 3 to 5 September 2005, and the second in Washington, DC, from 2 to 4 September 2006. The Toronto tournament was held at the Metro Convention Centre in the business district, approximately ten minutes south (by public transit) of Toronto's historic downtown Chinatown. The Washington tournament was also held at a parking lot and a convention centre, approximately five minutes' walking distance from Washington's downtown Chinatown. For these tournaments, I observed the three days of competition, a press conference, the opening ceremonies, the awards ceremony, and the Captains' Meeting. In addition, I observed two mini tournaments (in New York City, in July 2006; and in Mississauga, Ontario, Canada, in August 2015). The first, the New York Mini, was held in Manhattan, on the eastern side of Chinatown, and the second, the Phoenix Cup, was held at Rick Hansen Secondary School in Mississauga. I also observed the practices of one Toronto team during the summer of 2015.

Table 1.1   Information regarding interviewees

Pseudonym	Age at time of interview			"100% Chinese"	"Asian descent" (including "halfies")
	19–29	30–39	40+		
Adam			X		X
Amber	X			X	
Ava		X			X
Bill		X		X	
Brian	X				X
Carl			X	X	
Carol	X			X	
Christie	X				X
Cliff		X		X	
Diane	X			X	
Eli	X				X
Erin			X	X	
Graham			X	X	
Helen		X			X
Hugh		X		X	
Ira			X	X	
Irene	X				X
James		X			X
John	X				X
Karen	X				X
Ken			X	X	
Kyle	X			X	
Lisa		X		X	
Luke			X	X	
Mark	X				X
Michael			X	X	
Nancy	X			X	
Nick			X	X	
Owen			X	X	
Patrick		X		X	
Peter		X		X	
Phoebe	X			X	
Rachel	X			X	
Rob			X	X	
Sandy		X		X	
Sarah		X		X	
Steve		X		X	
Tom		X		X	
Vic			X	X	
Wendy		X		X	

Lastly, I analysed texts such as the tournament booklets that are distributed to participants (eight booklets, from 1999 to 2003, and from 2005 to 2007) and tournament websites (see the appendix). These sites provide key information to interested participants, such as details about the upcoming tournament, letters and statistics for sponsors, registration forms, social events, hotel news, and points of interest. Some websites also had space for users to comment. Other texts are listed in the appendix. I engaged in informal analysis, including noting the types of letters of support, advertising, photos, and languages that were used in the booklet, and recurring themes across the different tournament websites, paying particular attention to how community was constructed or assumed to be given, and the place or erasure of difference. I also considered the relationship of the texts to themes identified through the interview and participant-observation processes, marking potential contradictions and complexities.

The North American Chinese Invitational Volleyball Tournament

The North American Chinese Invitational Volleyball Tournament, which takes place on Labour Day weekend, attracts men's and women's teams from cities in Canada and the United States (and, on rare occasions, teams from abroad, such as Taiwan). It is usually held in one of five hosting cities: Toronto, Washington, San Francisco, New York, and Boston.[2] Local tournaments also occur

---

2 Montreal used to be one of the hosting cities; however, after 1998, teams in this city have been unable to host because of declining numbers and lack of support from the city's Chinatown(s). It hosted again in 2011 because of renewed interest in the NACIVT, particularly as it became known that a documentary film was being made about the tournament. Montreal hosted again in 2018. Los Angeles hosted the tournament in 2009 but has not become a regular part of the circuit. The 2014 tournament was scheduled to be in San Francisco but instead was organized in Las Vegas. In early 2017, it was announced that the tournament for that year would be held in Florida rather than Boston.

throughout the summer (e.g., the Canada Day tournament in Toronto; the New York Mini tournament in late July, and so on). Most teams play in competitive and adult recreational leagues and with other clubs during the regular volleyball season and/or begin practising for the NACIVT in May.

The NACIVT is known for "nine-man" volleyball, where there are nine rather than six players on the court. Little is known about the origins of the game or how the game spread to various cities and countries. Despite a search of public archives in Manhattan where the tournament is said to have officially begun, I was unable to find historical records or references to the NACIVT or nine-man. The Fédération Internationale de Volleyball (FIVB) states only that the nine-man rules originated in Japan in 1927 and were adopted by China later that same year ("Chronological highlights" n.d.). One source that is based on interviews with former players, including the first generation of NACIVT players, as well as personal collections of documents and photos, is "A Short History of Volleyball in Chinatown and the Annual North American Chinese Invitational Volleyball Tournament," published in the 55th Tournament booklet (1999). According to this history, nine-man volleyball began in Toisan, China, as a result of an adaptation of sixes volleyball that was introduced to China by missionaries from the United States. When Chinese men sojourned to work in the United States, they continued this pastime, with laundry workers in Boston taking the credit for being the first to play the game in the United States.[3]

Life was difficult for working-class people, and leisure time was extremely limited (Pan 1990). Chinese men faced considerable racism and threat of violence outside of Chinatown. They had limited resources and lived in poor and cramped housing. Sunday was the only day for recreation, one that was often spent in the company of other men, since anti-Chinese immigration legislation, racialized constructions of Chinese women as prostitutes, and miscegenation fears restricted the entry of Chinese women (C. Lee 2003). "A Short

---

3 No date is given, though presumably it is before 1935.

History" mirrors this description of working-class life when elaborating on the roots of the tournament:

> Recreation for laundry workers was extremely limited. Laundry work usually meant 10- to 18-hour days, 6 days a week. Sunday was their only day off. On Sunday they could do what they liked, but there was not much to do. [...] The facilities of the Chinatown Y were quite limited. There, the young men found a table tennis table and a backyard. In this backyard they could play volleyball. ("A short history" 1999, 22)

Volleyball was an ideal sport for laundry workers in Chinatown who did not have the means to purchase specialized equipment. Players improvised, using a rope or string in lieu of a net, marking out the boundaries of the court on the street or in alleyways, using stones or drawing lines, and fashioning a ball out of cloth instead of purchasing a volleyball. Such strategies were used in Toisan, China, from where many of the early migrants had arrived ("A short history" 1999; Liang 2014).

While this narrative has often been and continues to be reproduced and repeated, Michael (66 years old, first generation), a long-time NACIVT participant, was sceptical about this particular origins story. He had come to the United States at the age of 12 from Toisan, China, and did not recall seeing any Western missionaries during his childhood. Instead, he believed that it was Chinese sojourners who learned the game in the United States and taught it to locals upon their return to Toisan. This particular individual was considered one of the elders within the NACIVT community because of his many decades of involvement. Despite his status and the respect that he garnered, few seemed to question this dominant narrative of the invention of nine-man, and indeed, many repeated it to me in interviews, likely because this origins story was republished in almost every subsequent tournament booklet.

Matches between teams from Boston and Providence, Rhode Island, began in 1935. In 1937, people from New York also participated, and it became an annual event held in New York City. In 1939, Providence stopped competing because a team could no longer be supported. This gap was quickly filled by a team from

Newark, New Jersey. The game continued to spread to other cities through friends or family ties ("A short history" 1999). It is particularly significant that the early competitors were able to organize and travel to different cities, albeit nearby, to play and socialize with other Chinese American men. As Yep (2009) writes, the 1930s and 1940s were a time when "stringent institutional and cultural rules dictated and normalized ideas of where Chinese and Chinese Americans belonged and did not belong in America" (5). Laws were already in place that limited their movement across borders, such as the 1924 Immigration Exclusion Act, which limited opportunities to claim belonging in the United States because of the 1913 Alien Land Law that prevented land ownership and limited relationships through anti-miscegenation laws (Yep 2009; see also C. Lee 2003). Chinese and Chinese American people also encountered racial discrimination and violence, particularly if they left the boundaries of Chinatown (Yep 2009; see also Anderson 1987; C. Lee 2003). Negative stereotypes circulated via popular cultural representations, especially in relation to Chinatown, such as being unhygienic or the bearers of disease (e.g., Anderson 1987; Craddock 1999). Some of these representations continued into the twenty-first century, including being viewed as unassimilable, forever foreign, and mysterious (e.g., Millington, Vertinsky, Boyle, & Wilson 2008). At the same time Yep (2009) points out that in the late 1930s and 1940s, Chinese people in the United States were also characterized as benevolent, asexual, and non-threatening, perhaps because of the shift from the "yellow peril" to "good ally" status as a result of the Sino-Japanese War and the World War Two alliance between China and the United States. Ultimately, though, "discrimination kept Chinese Americans separate from mainstream America" (6), and this segregation was also evident in sports, as with the Chinese American basketball players in Yep's study. Her research participants, who actively participated in basketball around the same time that the first NACIVT teams began forming, rarely played against people of other racial backgrounds.

Washington teams joined the tournament in 1947 and San Francisco teams in 1971. The latter hosted their first tournament in

1974. The first Toronto team became involved that year and began hosting the tournament three years later, followed by Montreal in 1986. With the participation of Canadian teams, the tournament's name was changed from the Annual East Coast Volleyball Tournament to the North American Chinese Invitational Volleyball Tournament. So popular is the tournament that the 73rd tournament, held in 2017, had 121 men's and women's teams registered. Teams such as the New York Vikings, which was established in 1956, or the Boston Knights, which was formed in 1961 and was the first team of American-born Chinese, continue to participate.

The time period during which the NACIVT was forming, spreading to different cities, and attracting new teams coincides with a time when the Asian American movement was gaining momentum. Inspired by and drawing on other powerful social movements, such as the Black Power movement and anti-Vietnam war activism, the Asian American movement in the 1960s and 1970s sought to build a coalition across diverse ethnic groups and foster transnational solidarities (Maeda 2012). Specifically, a key project of the Asian American movement was to make the Asian American subject visible by pushing for recognition as a group and validation of the shared experiences of people of diverse backgrounds but who identified with the newly constructed category of "Asian American." In this endeavour, speaking from a position of being united by victimhood and vulnerability to racism proved to be an effective strategy in promoting a sense of solidarity (Espiritu 1992). In turn, this led to greater electoral influence, allowing Asian Americans to lobby for changes to social services and education.

Asian American activism on college and university campuses was also integral to the movement's success. In fact, a second important accomplishment of the movement was the establishment of ethnic studies and Asian American studies as scholarly disciplines and fields of study. Ono (2008) describes Asian American scholarship during its first phase (1971–97), as focusing primarily on a "nationalist project of self-definition and activism" (1), paralleling the principal focus of the broader Asian American movement. It was also consolidating the area of study as a field of inquiry. College and university students were critical to this achievement. Their activism served as an example of the interracial and transnational solidarities that in turn formed the foundation of the broader Asian American movement (Maeda 2012). Indeed, Maeda describes the role of these places of higher education "as incubators of Asian American action, places where students came together, were politicized, and built new identities and organizations" (27). While only one NACIVT team was formed with fellow university students (i.e., the New York Vikings) during that time period, it is conceivable that individuals who were attending college or university in the midst of the Asian American movement could have been influenced by or at the very least been aware of its mission and cause.

Asian Canadian research is not produced within an "Asian Canadian studies" department in the way that studies on Asians in the United States are, and this may explain the prevalence of literature on Asian Americans. Park (2007) observes that the bulk of the studies on Asians in Canada has been produced from the migration and settlement perspective, with a primary focus on the migration experience, such as barriers to integration, employment rates and barriers, education, intermarriage, residential patterns, and income levels (e.g., Fong & Ooka 2006; Lee & Boyd 2007; Li 1994; Li 2003a; Magee, Fong, & Wilkes 2007; Mitchell, 2004; Reitz 2001a, 2001b; Salaff, Greve, & Xu 2002). Like the initial focus of the Asian American movement, studies of Asians in Canada are also dominated by the project of highlighting the history of Asian exclusion and making the Asian subject visible within the Canadian nation space (Park 2007). In doing so, such studies produce the Asian Canadian subject as homogeneous, unified, and stable. A similar critique could also be made of early Asian American research and the early writings of Asian American activists. Thus, feminist writers argued that the way Asian American identity was being imagined was too masculinist (e.g., Pon 2000a), nationalist (e.g., Chuh 2003; Espiritu 1992; Lowe 1996), heterosexist (e.g., Eng & Hom 1998), and monoracial (Nakashima 2005).

There is an additional risk in constructing the Asian American or Asian Canadian subject in a narrow and homogeneous way. Following the dismantling of Asian exclusion laws in the 1940s and

1950s, opportunities for Asian American people expanded in terms of employment, neighbourhood, immigration, and citizenship, and with these new freedoms came the expectation for Asian Americans to perform and conform to the idea of the exemplary citizen or, in other words, "the model minority" (Wu 2013). The model minority myth is a stereotype that constructs Asians in both Canada and the United States as an ideal racial minority group because they have transcended discrimination and achieved success through hard work, diligence, and docility. They are presumed to be academically oriented and therefore not interested in the arts or sports (Maclear 1994; Mayeda 1991; Saito 1997). It is a stereotype that operates to celebrate Asian people while serving as a barrier for coalition building through indirectly disparaging other racialized groups. This trope emerged in the United States during the Cold War years as a way to reinforce assimilationist ideologies and to support US efforts to limit the influence of communism on non-Western countries through showcasing the success of racialized minorities as evidence of the success of US democracy (C.I. Cheng 2013).

The model minority myth was further consolidated through its appearance and the celebration of the Asian American as a model minority in mainstream media such as in the *New York Times* ("Orientals find bias is down sharply in US" 1970) and *Newsweek* ("Success story: Outwhiting the whites" 1970). Further, Wu (2013) argues that Japanese and Chinese Americans reinforced this myth by mobilizing stereotypical qualities such as being accommodating, having respect for family, valuing education, and having a strong work ethic. Such qualities, according to Wu, aligned nicely with liberal and integrationist imperatives and with American middle-class norms at the time. That an increasing number of Asian Americans were achieving well in education, employment, and overall upward mobility served as evidence of their model minority status. As a result of this narrow characterization, however, everyday racisms encountered by Asian people in Canada and the United States (Chou & Feagin 2015), racial triangulation and the subsequent construction of "bad" racial groups (e.g., Kim 1999; Wu 2013), and the socio-economic disparities among Asian American and Asian Canadian people are erased and ignored.

Personal narratives and experiences (e.g., Djao 2003; Goosen 1992; Sakamoto & Zhou 2005; Sugiman 2004) can help draw attention to different perspectives and to complex and contradictory lived realities, which in turn counter the model minority myth and a masculinist, nationalist, heterosexist, and monoracial Asian American and Asian Canadian identity. Such work therefore destabilizes the unified and stable Asian American or Asian Canadian subject and highlights, for instance, gendered stereotypes and the erasure of the diversity of Asian people's experiences. Nonetheless, Park (2007) suggests that such accounts remain stuck within a struggle for the "authentic" Asian and thus reinforce "Asianness" as essential and absolute. In a Canadian context these personal narratives are consumed as part of the celebration of multiculturalism, and the identity politics within which these stories arise is reduced to showcasing Canada's cultural mosaic (Park 2007). Furthermore, these narratives that try to capture the diversity of Asian Americans and Asian Canadians along gendered, geographic, and other lines often neglect physical cultural practices such as sports. It is significant therefore, that within a broader project of examining how Asianness is constituted, this book sheds light on Asian American and Asian Canadian women's participation in the NACIVT.

The women's division in the NACIVT began in 1977 after an exhibition game that was organized by a Boston tournament organizer who saw how female friends and girlfriends of players would volley or play keep-up during breaks in the official tournament play. They had learned sixes volleyball in high school physical education classes, and so their skill and technique were quite good. According to "A Short History" (1999), a long-time player from New York who organized a women's team contacted a representative of the Boston tournament and asked if there was a women's team in Boston that the team could play against. The organizer proceeded to put together a women's team, and an exhibition game was held during the subsequent Labour Day tournament in Boston. This game was scheduled immediately prior to the men's final championship in order to maximize attendance and interest. The women's game became a regular part of the tournament the following year in Toronto.

The women's division, though, follows the mainstream rules for volleyball, with six rather than nine players on the court. That women play sixes is rooted in sexist assumptions about sports being the domain of men and masculinity (Messner 1988), as reflected in the resistance against women's initial participation in the exhibition game in Boston, as well as ongoing views about the athletic (in)abilities of women and how women cannot achieve the height or power to complete the moves that are characteristic of the nines game (see chapter 3). Thus, not only are they not taught the nines game, they may be presumed to be unable to play it.

Women in the NACIVT play sixes because of both a lack of opportunity to learn to play nines and the abundant chances to learn and play sixes volleyball that are available through the public education system in Canada and the United States. According to the Volleyball Canada Development Model (n.d.), many athletes begin playing volleyball in high school and compete through inter-school competitions, and then through the club system during the summer. Unfortunately, there are limited Canadian data on girls' and women's participation in volleyball. Based on a report on the status of female sports participation in Canada, 22 per cent of girls between the ages of 3 and 17 years participate in a team sport; volleyball was ninth out of the top ten organized sports in which girls participate (Canada's Dairy Farmers & CAAWS 2016). According to the Ontario Volleyball Association (2015), among youth 13 to 18 years of age, girls' participation in Ontario constitutes approximately 75 per cent of their athlete demographic. The popularity of volleyball among women improves in adulthood, with volleyball being fourth out of the top ten sports in which Canadian women participate (Canadian Heritage 2013), with approximately 7 per cent of female sports participants playing volleyball. In comparison, approximately 9 per cent of male sports participants played volleyball. While the overall percentages of participants appear low, volleyball remains relatively popular, and it is likely that girls and women have sufficient opportunities to play volleyball in Canada.

In the case of volleyball in the United States, the sport is dominated by women. According to USA Volleyball (2007), in the general population, 61.4 per cent of volleyball players are female, compared to 28.6 per cent of players who are male. Among USA Volleyball members, 86.1 per cent of its members are female. Furthermore, over the course of twenty-six years, Junior Female membership in USA Volleyball has steadily increased from approximately 10,000 in 1986 to approximately 150,000 in 2006, while Junior Male membership has remained stable at around 10,000. These data are drawn from a survey conducted by Sport Management Institute at the University of Northern Colorado (2007) and the Superstudy of Sports Participation (2005) (as cited by USA Volleyball 2007). Not surprisingly, a High School Athletics Participation Survey found that in the 2014–15 school year, 54,418 boys at 2,287 schools played volleyball compared to 432,176 girls at 15,534 schools (National Federation of State High School Associations 2014–15). There is a clear disparity between the number of girls playing volleyball compared to boys, as well as between the number of schools that have a girls' volleyball team compared to those that have a boys' volleyball team. At the college level, the popularity of volleyball remains high, with 96 per cent of National Collegiate Athletic Association (NCAA) schools having a women's volleyball team, second only to basketball (American Volleyball Coaches Association 2015). It is evident, therefore, that girls and women in the United States have many opportunities to develop their skills in sixes volleyball, and this helps to explain the high level of competence of the US women's teams in the NACIVT. It does make one wonder why girls and women with ample opportunity to play volleyball in the United States would be interested in competing in the NACIVT. What is it about the NACIVT that attracts Asian American and Asian Canadian female volleyball players?

The cost of participating in the tournament varies each year. This difference is largely related to the venue for the tournament. Indoor tournaments, such as the 68th Toronto tournament held at the Metropolitan Toronto Convention Centre, are more expensive because of rental costs. The registration fees for the 70th tournament held indoors at the Westgate Resort and Casino in Las Vegas were $800 USD and $1,000 USD for the women's and men's teams, respectively, with an additional $200 USD security deposit, and an extra $200 USD for late registration. Players must also consider the cost of transportation, accommodation, and food. In some cases, clubs engage in fundraising activities to cover the cost of food during the event and a few nights of accommodation. Group rates at hotels are often arranged by the tournament organizers, such as $130 CAD per night for the 2012 68th Toronto tournament and $90 USD per night for the 2015 70th Las Vegas tournament (plus a $200 security deposit). Many interviewees mentioned that they would maximize or exceed the number of people who could stay in one room in order to lessen the cost of the trip.

Likely related to the increasing cost of participation and the changing demographic of more recent immigrants from China and other Asian countries, the overall class backgrounds of NACIVT players have changed from their working-class roots. In a Letter to Sponsors written by the 2006 Washington tournament organizing committee, the annual income levels of participants were estimated as follows: between $45,001 and $100,000 – 39 per cent; between $100,001 and $175,000 –35 per cent; and more than $175,000 – 18 per cent (62nd NACIVT 2006). While this demographic information was taken from a small sample, it suggests that approximately 50 per cent of players are making more than $100,000, well above the low-income cut-off threshold in Canada (i.e., in 2017: $24, 600 for an individual; $45,712 for a family of four) and the poverty thresholds in the United States (i.e., in 2017: $12,752 for an individual under age 65; $25,283 for a family of four). By comparison, the average income of Canadians of Chinese origin aged 15 and over was about $25,000 in 2000 (Statistics Canada 2006) and, for Chinese aged 16 and over in the United States, $38,000 in 2015 (PEW Research Center 2017), with a median income of $66,000 for Asian Americans overall (PEW Research Center 2012). Although the Letter to the Sponsors includes a caveat that this breakdown of income is an estimate and reflects a small group of players, the relative financial comfort of the participants is corroborated in another Letter to Sponsors, this time seeking to fundraise for a friendship tourney to China. In it, the players are described as "professional lawyers, physicians, engineers and other professional people" (*New York Mini* 2006). While many Chinese Americans are professionals and have a higher income than the national per-capita average (Hune 2002), the league demographics are not representative of Chinese or Asian Americans and Canadians in general. Clearly, there has been a marked shift away from the tournament's working-class origins.

Even beyond the seemingly upward change in the NACIVT participants' class status, there is a culture of middle classness among the players. For instance, interviewees implied that fundraising is not a financial necessity but a team-building opportunity and a chance to socialize. For younger players who may not be able to pay for tournaments on their own, it is assumed that their parents will pay. When financial constraints *are* recognized, they are framed as something that one outgrows or overcomes with age, reinforcing the assumption of middle-class homogeneity and of economic barriers as temporary rather than structural. In addition, the physical and corporeal experience of playing volleyball exemplifies the ethos of self-help among middle-class cultures, in terms of the relationship between the body and sports (Bourdieu 1978). The interviewees, for example, spoke of gaining tremendous satisfaction from intense practices and of the pleasure of training for the NACIVT. Many of the serious clubs and teams in fact begin practices in May, renting gymnasiums at local schools. Once the weather improves, teams sometimes move outdoors and practise in parking lots, all with a focus on the Labour Day tournament in September.

The disconnect between the working-class history and the contemporary culture of the tournament became very clear to me during a shuttle-bus ride to the Grand Hyatt, the tournament-affiliated hotel in Washington, for the 2006 tournament. I was sharing the van with four other travellers, who, based on their conversation, were travelling on a tight budget. As the van waited to make a turn into the hotel roundabout, they each marvelled at the grandeur of the hotel, wondered aloud who was staying there, and wished they could stay there too. Indeed, at the two Labour Day tournaments I attended, the remnants of working-class culture out of which the NACIVT arose could only be found among the maintenance and security staff of the convention centres in Toronto and Washington, the restaurant workers who serve food in Chinatown where the players eat, and the staff of the hotels where players stay. Indeed, the salience of class within the NACIVT is mostly diminished, except among the people who labour on Labour Day weekend so that others may play, in the retelling of the NACIVT history, and among the few working-class players who are recent immigrants from Toisan, China. Nonetheless, the history of marginalization and working-class struggles in which the NACIVT is rooted serve as a critical foundation upon which contemporary exclusions via the eligibility rules are justified (chapter 2).

The rules on player eligibility state that while at least two-thirds of the players must be "100 per cent Chinese," a maximum of one-third of the players on the court may be of Asian descent (see chapter 2 for full eligibility rules). Half-Chinese or 50 per cent Chinese players (i.e., those who have one parent who is Chinese) are also included in the Asian category. These rules, according to one long-time participant and alumnus, were put in place in 1991. Prior to the implementation of these rules, there do not appear to have been any specific, codified regulations regarding who was permitted to play. In fact, retired players recalled competing with players who were neither Chinese nor Asian, and that mixed-race or mixed-ethnicity Chinese players were not limited in their playing opportunities.

Historically, the tournament took place in the streets of downtown Chinatowns. The reason for this, as interviewees often repeated, is that early Chinese Americans were not permitted access to physical activity and sports spaces (see chapter 2; Nakamura 2012). More recently, tournaments have been taking place in and around various Chinatowns, such as Seward Park on the eastern edge of Manhattan's Chinatown, and a parking lot a few blocks from Washington, DC's Chinatown. Interestingly, in 2013, the NACIVT in Washington, DC, was held on Pennsylvania Avenue with a number of historic American federal buildings serving as backdrop (see photo 2.1). However, with the increasing popularity and institutionalization of the event, the tournament sites have moved indoors into public venues – for example, convention centres, as in Toronto (2005), Washington (2007), and Las Vegas (2014).

The first day of the 2005 NACIVT in Toronto, for instance, used approximately 200,000 square feet of space in the Metropolitan Toronto Convention Centre.

If games are not played in a gymnasium, the lines of the court are marked with duct tape, and there may also be a mesh hung between sections to limit wayward balls from entering other courts. The posts holding the nets are kept in place by several cinder blocks piled high or by barrels of water on wooden pallets. At the 2015 Phoenix Cup, nets were held in place by participants' cars. A chair, step stool, or ladder is placed by one of the poles where the referee stands. There is a Control Table where the tournament awards are sometimes on display and where teams can find play schedules, court allocations, work schedules (for those acting as officials for games), and team rosters.

As teams enter the tournament venue, they scout out a space that will be home for the next three days. In outdoor venues, the teams set up tents and lawn chairs, arrange coolers, listen to music to get into a game-ready mindset, or pull out their volleyballs. Some teams even have tables and portable barbeques to prepare hamburgers and hot dogs during the lunch break, while other teams begin organizing lunch orders for parents, older players, or alumni to pick up. Soon, a hundred or more volleyballs are in the air, as players finish setting up their space and begin warming up. The only time the balls are still is when the American and Canadian national anthems are being played.

Each match begins with the same general routine: the teams warm up on their respective sides; then one team practises using the whole court, after which they make way for the opposing team to do the same. Unique to the nine-man game is that, at the referee's signal, players line up at the back of the court, bow to the opposing team, and then proceed to jog along the outside boundary, greet opposing players at the net, and then return to their side of the court to do a team cheer. The starting line-up gets ready, and at the sound of the whistle the first serve is delivered and the game begins. The players focus on the game, while coaches and bench players provide instruction, feedback, and support from the sidelines. Teams frequently huddle together after each play, either to celebrate a point or to help one another to recover from an error or point taken. It is not unusual for players on the receiving team to be poised to accept the serve, knees bent, arms and hands extended, and eyes trained on the ball and the serving player. The intensity of the matches is undeniable. Players frequently smack the ball, clap their hands together, or swear loudly in frustration, even during a practice. On one occasion, I was startled when a player who was on a court on the other side of the gym, cursed loudly, and slapped his hands on the floor, the loud sound echoing throughout the gym. A documentary film (Liang 2014) of the tournament captures this intensity, with one particular scene of some players angrily contesting a call, their chests puffed out while yelling at the referee.

Teams are clearly distinguished from one another by their uniforms, although players may not have common attire if their team has come together at the last minute. Some teams wear cotton t-shirts with team names and logos, while others wear moisture-wicking athletic shirts emblazoned with their team names, logos, player numbers, and sponsors. Some teams even have matching shorts as part of their uniforms, while other teams only have common shirts. In general, the men's uniforms are baggy shorts, a t-shirt or tank top, athletic socks, and running shoes. A number of players wear padding on their knees and athletic tape on various parts of their bodies, including their fingers. Sunglasses, visors, or hats are also common. The women also wear t-shirts or tank tops, athletic socks, and running shoes. They too often wear knee and elbow pads, and athletic tape. Women typically wear tight spandex shorts that come slightly below the buttocks, similar to the FIVB-mandated uniforms for elite level women volleyball players. It is rare to see women wearing baggy shorts, track pants, or even leggings. Long hair is usually pulled back in ponytails and stray hair is kept at bay with a hairband. Unlike Chin's (2012) research study of Japanese American basketball leagues where the women players had a standard hair clip as part of their uniform, no women's teams at the tournaments I observed had such mandated accessories.

Because there are several matches taking place at the same time, the tournament atmosphere is not quiet. It is typical to hear the smack of open palms spiking a ball, the blowing of whistles, whoops of celebration, screaming for the ball, and the cheering of fans. The men's voices tend to be lower and louder, especially since the men's teams are larger than the women's teams, though the shouts of women can still be heard. Even at a practice, I had a hard time hearing and often had to yell when speaking to the person beside me. The close quarters and limited partitions mean that balls from other matches or players warming up can enter the court, temporarily stopping the play. Fans sit close to the lines, even beside the scorekeepers. Thus, spectators have to pay close attention in order to deflect, retrieve, and return balls, as well as to avoid players who come running out of bounds in an attempt to save an errant ball, sometimes crashing into a distracted observer. Indeed, when I was attending a practice of a Toronto team in the summer of 2015, I was so engrossed in my note-taking that I did not notice that there was a volleyball hurtling towards me until it had hit me squarely in the head and then knocked my pen and notebook out of my hand! In general, spectators are other competitors in the tournament, with, for example, the men's team supporting the women's team from the same club, or teams supporting one another if they are from the same city. Friends, partners, and family members also sit on the sidelines, cheering a team on. There is no obvious difference between the numbers of men versus women on the sidelines. The only striking discrepancy in spectators is the degree of support for the men's championship match as compared to the women's; the men's match enjoys a much bigger audience.

The playing schedule is organized as a round robin[4] to maximize participation, which is especially important for teams that travel long distances. In general, the format of the tournament involves a large pool of teams that is then gradually separated into different tiers of skill and competitive levels. Each team competes within

---

4 A round robin in sports refers to a format where each team plays against every other team, with the winner emerging from the succession of bouts.

a single pool of teams and must win two out of three matches in order to advance. The top-tier teams and lower-ranked teams are separated into two different pools, the Power Pool and the Challenger Pool, in the case of the 2016 NACIVT in Los Angeles. There are three different brackets, Gold, Silver, and Bronze, to which teams advance as they win or lose against other teams. Once the three brackets are determined, teams need to win two out of three matches in order to advance, although this sometimes shifts, depending on how much time remains in the tournament. If, for example, a tourney is running behind schedule, then the organizers may choose to make the first round a single-elimination or sudden-death game where a losing team is immediately eliminated. Later, the organizers may switch back to a best-two-out-of-three format.

As each day progresses, there are fewer and fewer teams playing as the championship pool begins to be whittled down. By the second day of the 2006 Toronto tournament, only two of the exhibition halls were used. As teams advance further into the playoffs, the intensity of play and the interest of fans increase. When it is time for the men's championship match, fans may be standing five people deep. While interest may not be as high for the women's championship, the passion with which the women play is palpable.

Overview of This Book

Idealized terms like "community," "tradition," and "authenticity"; historical roots in working-class and Asian migrant cultures; and repeated narratives of marginalization and disenfranchisement combine with the contemporary culture of middle classness and provide a backdrop for how identity and belonging are understood within the NACIVT. They also serve as a foundation that stabilizes these constructs, and erases difference. In what follows, I investigate the processes through which belonging and community are constructed, particularly the strategies of exclusion and inclusion that rely on notions of race, gender, and culture. Throughout the text, I emphasize this duality through deliberate capitalization of racialized terms, and through the use of quotation marks, to indicate when terms are being deployed in ways that assume stability but are in flux. Chapter 2 investigates processes of racial boundary-making that continually produce difference and that make the community being constructed seem unchanging and homogeneous. The subsequent processes of excluding difference and hierarchizing Others are grounded in the notion of biological essentialism, which is deployed via race, gender, and culture (chapter 3). Chapter 4 examines how community is constructed, in response to internal differences, through the passing of traditions from one generation to the next and the making of new traditions across difference. The book finishes with an epilogue, revisiting the NACIVT almost a decade after I first began studying the tournament, and discussing what the future holds.

Photo 1.1 Toronto Connex and PHI CIA, 2018, New York. A middle hitter performs a step-around/slide hit from a Philadelphia CIA player. Credit: Rosanna U.

Photo 1.2 Montreal Freemasons and PHI CIA, 2018, New York. A Montreal Freemason player attempts to swing on the ball. Three Philadelphia CIA players attempt to block. Credit: Rosanna U.

Photo 1.3 Toronto Flying Tigers and LA iVball, 2013, Washington. A Toronto Flying Tigers player demonstrates a power attack. Two LA iVball players form a block. Credit: Andrea Park.

Photo 1.4 New York Strangers and Connex, 2018, New York. A Strangers player attacks from the fastball position. Three Connex players attempt to block. Blockers are careful not to penetrate the imaginary net line, a rule unique to nine-man. Credit: Rosanna U.

Chapter 2

"There's a Line, and We're Going to Keep That Line": Boundaries of Belonging

In the critically acclaimed documentary film *9-man*, filmmaker Ursula Liang interviews Jeff Chung, a player and coach with a long history with nine-man volleyball and its annual championship competition, the North American Chinese Invitational Volleyball Tournament (NACIVT). Liang (2014) likely chose to interview him because he is well known among the tournament participants, greatly respected, and highly regarded for his volleyball skills and his success as an athlete, both in the tournament and beyond. In one scene, Chung is shown staring back at Liang, who is off camera, and stating without hesitation that "It is flattering that other cultures want to get involved, but there's a line, and we're going to keep that line." He is referring to the NACIVT's eligibility rules and the question of including ethnic, cultural, and racial groups other than those identified in the tournament's official eligibility rules. Chung's position is clear. There is a boundary that cannot be crossed. Those who are perceived not to belong may not enter this community and participate in the tournament; this is not going to change. Chung is not alone in this view. The eligibility rules delineate the boundaries of belonging within the tournament, and those who uphold them engage in boundary work that is justified by socially constructed ideas of ethnic and racial belonging (see chapter 3). While Chung may be definitive in his view that this boundary is real and is steadfastly to be maintained, there are in fact multiple boundaries that operate within the NACIVT, and their existence is not given but is being actively produced. Further, the boundaries are frequently crossed.

The line that Chung wishes to keep surrounds a community that in his mind shares a culture that is different from those Others who wish to participate in the NACIVT. His desire to maintain "the line" or boundary reflects a desire to protect a sense of community, a commonly shared value among the NACIVT participants I interviewed. One of the most important elements of participation in the NACIVT is belonging to a community that is cultivated via relationships with other players and the sense of support received through these relationships (see chapter 4), an emphasis seen in other leagues and sports that are organized along ethnic or religious lines (e.g., Chin 2016; Walseth 2006). The NACIVT certainly facilitates relationships between people who share an interest in volleyball, physical activity, winning, being part of a team, and working towards self- and team improvement. That volleyball is a team sport would foster a sense of commitment and responsibility to one another (see also Chin 2016). Thus, the NACIVT community aligns with Bruhn's definition of community in that it is a site of support, companionship, social interaction, and positive ties with others that give meaning to our lives. People within the NACIVT community may share similar goals, values, and perhaps a lifestyle that creates positive feelings and a sense of mutual commitment and responsibility to one another (Bruhn 2005). These relationships and networks can lead to other opportunities and the sharing of cultural capital (e.g., Chin 2016; see also Nakamura 2016).

Nevertheless, the eligibility rules and the position that Chung takes in Liang's documentary highlight that the NACIVT community is understood in terms of the boundary that keeps difference out and is, therefore, a community premised on exclusion and how Otherness is constructed (Gupta & Ferguson 1992). When Others are excluded, boundaries of community may be carefully watched "so that the uniqueness of the culture and solidarity of its members can be retained" (Bruhn 2005, 12). Thus, it is imperative that we examine "diaspora's borders ... what it defines itself against" (Clifford 1997, 250).

"Diaspora" is a term that is frequently used in a general way to encompass a wide range of people, such as expatriates, those in exile, refugees, alien residents, immigrants, and all ethnic and racial minorities (Braziel & Mannur 2003; Brubaker 2005; Safran 1991). Its contemporary usage, therefore, has become vacuous, ranging from references to the exile, subsequent dispersion, and oppression of Jewish people to a current use that includes anyone who undertakes a migration journey. To re-establish and maintain the critical and theoretical utility of the term "diaspora," Brah writes that scholars must "be attentive to the nature and type of processes in and through which the collective 'we' is constituted" (Brah 1996, 184). Theorizing diaspora therefore does not take the collectivity as given but instead asks how it is produced, who is empowered and disempowered, how social divisions are negotiated, what is the relationship of this collectivity to Others (Brah 1996), and what is the *lived experience*, with all its contradictory and ambivalent dimensions, of people within various diasporic communities (Braziel & Mannur 2003). Such an approach avoids an atheoretical understanding of diaspora that sees scattered people as connected by a common history, heritage, or race, and in turn evades ethnic absolutism, essentializing, and the presumed utopia of diaspora (Braziel & Mannur 2003). Furthermore, by thinking of diaspora as a collectivity that is *produced*, we can identify the difference, or Otherness, against which this construction occurs, as well as the boundaries between the two.

A key step then in using diaspora as the lens through which to understand the community that is being constructed by NACIVT participants is to identify how difference is presumed to be kept out or, in other words, the process through which boundaries are produced. In the case of the NACIVT, there is first a racial boundary that operates, one that reflects "relations of power, in particular, the ability of the dominant group to construct and impose definitions upon others" (Kibria 1998, 941). The relations of power that draw the racial boundaries of the NACIVT include the limits placed on Chinese people through the Head Tax, the Chinese Exclusion Act (in the United States), the Chinese Immigration Act (in Canada), the construction of Chinatowns (e.g., Anderson 1987; Craddock 1999), Japanese American and Japanese Canadian internment, anti-Asian racism and violence, and the marking of

Chinese and other Asian people as diseased during the epidemic of Severe Acute Respiratory Syndrome (SARS). SARS was an illness that broke out between 2002 and 2004 and afflicted 8,000 people from various countries. Despite its global spread, once the origin of the illness was identified to be China, people of Chinese descent in Canada were greatly stigmatized, experiencing discrimination and racism (Leung & Guan 2004). In fact, around the world, as a result of how the disease was portrayed in the media, Asian people encountered racial discrimination, alienation, and stigmatization (K. Lee 2013).

There is an additional dimension of power that works to define racial boundaries, one that differentiates between "100 per cent" Chinese and those of mixed-race Chinese background, identifying the latter as "less than"; that differentiates Asian from Chinese; and that identifies half-Asian as Other. These boundaries operate through the social construction of blood, race, and identity and are evident in how the eligibility rules are articulated and deployed. The specific rules are found in sections M3.0 and W2.0 of the rules governing the men's and women's games. The wording in both sections is the same:

> All teams must have at least 2/3 of the players on the court at all times who are 100% Chinese in order to participate in any of the games of the tournament. The remaining players must be of Asian descent. Asian players that had competed in prior tournament(s) (before 1991) on an established team are exempted from the 2/3 limitation requirement stated above and are permitted to play at any time. Any questions regarding the eligibility of any player must be presented before a game to the Tournament Committee. Once the game starts, the game becomes official and non-contestable. At the request of the Tournament Committee, any competitor may be required to show proof of compliance to the above requirement.
>
> Burden of proof shall be the responsibility of the player. If, in the opinion of the Committee that [sic] the protest is valid, the player will not be eligible to play and/or said team will be required to modify its line-up. In the event that a protest cannot be satisfactor[il]y resolved,

the protest can be submitted to the National Tournament Committee for decision. The decision of the National Tournament Committee will be final.

(Asian – origins from: Myanmar (formerly Burma), Cambodia, China, Hong Kong, Indonesia, Japan, Korea, Laos, Malaysia, Mongolia, Philippines, Singapore, Taiwan, Thailand, Vietnam)

* Mongolia added 57th NACIVT, effective 58th NACIVT.
* Burma notation updated to Myanmar.

(*Rules and eligibility* 2007)

Asian origins, according to the rules, do not include South Asian. In fact, a few South Asian players have attempted to participate during the main Labour Day Tournament, only to be prevented from stepping onto the court or asked not to return in subsequent tournaments, although their involvement in local tournaments, where the stakes are not as high, is ignored or dismissed. This is quite different from Thangaraj's (2015a) ethnography of South Asian American basketball participation, whose findings show how some of the subjects in his study could participate in multi-ethnic and multiracial basketball settings, such as Asian American basketball leagues.

These types of rules are not unique to the NACIVT. For example, within the Japanese American basketball leagues and tournaments in southern California in Willms's (2010) study, there are guidelines of eligibility that were based on racial or ethnic background. Nevertheless, some organizers were more flexible with their inclusion criteria, "making exceptions for those belonging to community organizations" (93). On the other hand, the Japanese American youth basketball league in Chin's (2012) study did not have official rules regarding non-Japanese players. However, there was a strong preference for individuals of Japanese ancestry, such that recruitment was through word of mouth and through the Youth Summer Basketball Camp where active recruitment of non-Asians did not take place. If a league board member was ever approached, Chin noted that individuals without Japanese or at the very least Asian ancestry would be directed to the city-based league instead. While not a sports example, Japanese American beauty pageants also have racial/ancestry-based eligibility criteria for participation (King-O'Riain 2006).

While the NACIVT eligibility rules do not limit participating as a volunteer, spectator, coach, fan, passerby, parent, partner, sponsor, or organizer, players are limited in terms of ethnicity and race by this eligibility rule. Because these boundaries are enacted upon players, they are only in effect during moments of play. However, as illustrated in subsequent sections, these rules have significant and often painful effects, and act to construct hierarchies among the players because the restrictions are closely related to how membership is defined and how circumstances of exclusion are determined and justified.

Chinese origins are not explicitly defined in the eligibility rules, while Asian origins are. Chinese can include those who have migrated to Canada and the United States via other diasporic nodes such as Hong Kong, Taiwan, India, or various parts of Africa and the Caribbean. The assumption that China is the ultimate homeland of individuals within the Chinese diaspora demonstrates how relationship to a homeland continues to shape this particular community and define who is and is not Chinese. Interestingly, Hong Kong and Taiwan are explicitly named under Asian origins, but Tibet is not. At the time the original eligibility rules were written, the transfer of sovereignty over Hong Kong from the United Kingdom to China had not taken place. Furthermore, US and Taiwan relations had been ambiguous, while Canada had recognized the One China Policy (see Nakamura 2016). The People's Republic of China is explicit in its position that Tibet is an inseparable part of China, a position that essentially has been supported by US and Canadian foreign policies, and this may be reflected in the invisibility of Tibet within the rules.

Those who have only one Chinese parent are considered 50 per cent Chinese. In such instances, these individuals may only constitute up to one-third of the line-up, along with the Asian players, be they mixed race or 100 per cent Asian. Thus, a player whose parents are both Chinese (defined as tracing origins back to China) would still fall into the 100 per cent Chinese category even if she identified as Jamaican, for example. Or a person who has one parent who is deemed Chinese, according to the rules, would be considered 50 per cent Chinese, regardless of whether the player self-identifies as Chinese. Players who have Asian parents, as defined by the rules, would be considered 100 per cent Asian, whether both are Filipino or one parent is Korean and the other is Malaysian. Someone who has an Indonesian mother and a Turkish father would be categorized as 50 per cent Asian. Relying on this idea of blood-quantum is not unique to the NACIVT and can be seen in Japanese American beauty pageants and basketball leagues. It is a racial recipe which assumes "that the amount of blood denotes ancestry and that ancestry is divided into biological parts" (King-O'Riain 2006, 188).

The eligibility rules did not come into existence until the early 1990s. Despite what a number of interviewees believed, in the beginning there was no rule that dictated who could and could not play. Michael, a former player from the United States, first began participating in the 1950s, shortly after graduating from a prestigious university in the United States. Michael claimed that because they did not know of any "non-Asians" who had an interest in playing, "it was never a factor that we said together, let's not have any non-Asian play." What is left unsaid is that Michael had started playing at a time when Chinese American people were viewed with suspicion because of the establishment of the People's Republic of China (PRC) and anti-communist anxieties that were increasing in the United States at the time. Thus, friendly and regular encounters between Michael and "non-Asians" and expressions of curiosity and interest in engaging in a Chinese activity like the NACIVT may have been few and far between.

Michael also recalled a time when a "Caucasian player" participated and nobody objected: "We could object, but, hey, that's the fun. He's not a superstar. By one person, he cannot dominate the game. So we let him play. Never thought anything about it." Had he been a superstar who dominated the game, Michael's views might have been different. Indeed, only when the presence of "non-Asians" became too prevalent or "got outtahand" (Michael) were

the eligibility rules codified and boundaries defined. Another interviewee recalled that shortly before the codification, one championship team had a number of strong Japanese players and speculated
that this was the catalyst for the implementation of the eligibility rules. This observation has all the more significance within an
increasingly competitive environment where the desire to win was
overshadowing the ethos of playing for fun. What becomes clear is
that the belonging that was to be cultivated through the NACIVT
is premised on agreement that it is Chineseness that is the central
point of reference that determines who may participate, to what
extent, and their position within the community. Ultimately, the
rules institutionalize the construction of the NACIVT as an expression of Chinese physicality and physical culture, with other Asian
sporting bodies serving as support on the path to victory.

While the social and political context leading up to the introduction and implementation of the eligibility rules was not mentioned by the interviewees, it is helpful to consider it. In both
Canada and the United States, for example, the model minority
thesis was increasingly based on the success that Asian immigrants
and their children were achieving (see chapter 1). Nevertheless, in
the 1980s, there was also an increasing degree of violence against
Asian American people (Kim 1999). For example, in 1982, two men
who held anti-Japanese sentiments beat Vincent Chin, a Chinese
American, to death in Detroit. Thus, the racial difference of Asians
in the United States continued to be entrenched, even with a simultaneous "positive" view of Asian American people. Even in the
sporting context, Kristi Yamaguchi, an American figure skater of
Japanese background, was consistently represented in US sports
media in a way that emphasized her Japanese (read: foreign) roots
(Kim 1999). The decade prior to the implementation of the eligibility
rules also coincides with a time period of Asian American activism.
Espiritu identifies Chin's murder as almost the moment of birth
of Asian American panethnicity (see chapter 3). This panethnicity
had support in Canada (Espiritu 1992), but it seems that in Canada
there was more ethnicity-based political organizing than in the
United States. For example, in 1979, a national news show known
as CTV W5 aired an episode that claimed that "foreigners" were

taking away spots from non-Chinese Canadian students in universities. In response, the Chinese Canadian National Council (CCNC) was formed to organize the Chinese Canadian community around this negative representation. This led to a public apology from the broadcasting company (CCNC n.d.).

Other events around the time of the rule changes are the redress campaigns and ultimate compensation to Japanese Americans and Japanese Canadians who were interned during World War Two. They received from their respective governments a formal apology and recognition of this injustice. The month of May was also designated as Asian Pacific American Heritage month in the United States, a celebration that has since been taken up in Canada as well. In light of the broader context where there is a move to unite Asian American people, it seems contradictory that the captains at the pre-tournament meeting in Washington in 1989 would adopt rules that hierarchize "Asian" people in the NACIVT. However, the move reflects the diverse reality of the Asian American movement, the conflicts and inequities that a unified front attempted to mask and ignore, and the specific sporting context in which the eligibility rules operate.

The eligibility rules have been amended over the years, as illustrated by the addition of Mongolia. Any changes to the rules must be proposed at the Captains' Meeting, which takes place the evening before the tournament. If changes are approved, these amendments take effect during the subsequent tournament. According to the previous nacivt.com website, at one point, the provision of the unlimited playing time of "non-Chinese Asian" players who have participated prior to 1991, known as the "grandfather clause," was removed. This clause is similar to one in the Japanese American basketball league studied by Willms (2010), where anyone of any racial or ethnic background could participate and could continue playing with that team or league for as long as they wished, provided they had started before a certain age. The NACIVT grandfather clause was taken out because it was assumed that most people to whom the rule would apply had retired and were no longer playing in the tournament. Three years later, the grandfather clause was reintroduced "by a vote of 21–6 at the Toronto 2000

Tournament" (*Women rules and regulations* n.d.). The reason for this change was neither explained in the official history reproduced in the tournament booklets nor understood by older members of the NACIVT who were interviewed.

Despite the laundry list of who counts as "Asian," there is no similarly explicit definition of "mixed-race Asian" people. Some interviewees seemed to think that "non-Chinese Asian" players must be at a minimum "50 per cent Asian" – or in other words have one parent who is "Asian" – to be permitted to play. However, there have been players who have only one grandparent who is "Asian" (i.e., they are "25 per cent Asian"), or in the case of one interviewee, a great-grandparent who is "Asian." At the 2008 NACIVT, a player claimed that he was one-sixteenth Asian. The person who shared this story with me indicated that this player did not "look Asian at all" but was permitted to play because he brought "paperwork" that supported his claim to "Asianness." What this paperwork was, he did not know, but it was deemed sufficient to allow this one-sixteenth Asian player to participate. Other interviewees also mentioned documentation to prove one's eligibility, including copies of passports or citizenship papers of players and their family members, whereby last name, place of birth, and photos are used as evidence of one's Asianness. Unlike King-O'Riain's (2006) beauty pageant participants who were mixed-race Japanese American and who used ethnic strategies to claim racial belonging (e.g., speaking Japanese, competing using their Japanese names), the mixed-race participants in the NACIVT assert racial belonging by offering various forms of evidence, evidence that relies on the conflation of race, ethnicity, citizenship, ancestry, place of birth, and phenotype.

Drawing Boundaries

The official eligibility rules are reinforced from the outset of the Labour Day tournament. Specifically, to register for the tournament, each team must submit a roster that includes players' names, uniform numbers, and ethnicity, including percentage breakdown, such as "100 per cent Chinese," "50 per cent Asian," and so on. These forms are compiled and left at the control table if players wish to confirm which players are or are not "100 per cent Chinese" and ensure that their opponents have a legal line-up. So important is this information that Amber described the binder containing the forms as "a Bible." During the 2007 tournament, organizers provided copies of the rosters at each court so that this information was readily accessible, a move that was applauded later (6 September 2007) by participants (NACIVT-SF n.d.).

Boundaries are reinforced in other more informal and implicit ways throughout the course of the tournaments. For example, those who are not "100 per cent Chinese" are marked as Other by calling them "alien" (Karen), of "Oriental descent" (John), "non-content" (Nancy), "illegal" (Brian), or "illegit" (Karen). These are the terms that players used to describe themselves and those in the tournament. Some players were more concerned with the boundary between "Asian" and "non-Asian." Diane felt that while being exclusively Chinese was discriminatory, drawing the boundary at "Asian" was more inclusive and still allowed for the NACIVT to retain its uniqueness. Similarly, James welcomed anyone who was "Asian" or "part Asian" to his team and did not actively police the border of "Chinese" and "non-Chinese Asian." Nevertheless, neither Diane nor James was critical of or questioned how "Chinese" and "Asian" were socially constructed.

A frequent way in which boundaries are reinforced is through the assessment of an individual player's eligibility. Amber, for example, recalled how players and teams "always ask, 'Are you 100 per cent Chinese?'" This information would be gleaned while playing against and socializing with other players and later used during a match to assess whether teams and players are following the eligibility rules. For teams and players that are new to the tournament, players on the court are likely assessed as to whether they are sufficiently within the confines of the boundaries laid out by the eligibility rules. One interviewee recalled, for example, that despite not being Chinese, early in her career when she was not well known, her coach sometimes attempted to "pass" her off as "100 per cent Chinese" on the court. On these occasions, she would sometimes be pointed out by opposing players and deemed ineligible to be on the court. In cases where players were new to the tournament or whose identities were deemed "ambiguous," their bodies would be read and racialized to determine their eligibility. In particular, those people whose bodies are read as "half" or "mixed" are placed under heightened scrutiny.

I use the phrase "reading and racializing bodies" to refer to the process of reading the body as a text and the way in which certain markers of this text are then racialized such that the body is assigned to occupy real and static racial groupings. Carrington (2002), for example, provides a detailed examination of how the "Black" body is read and meant to signify certain ideas and meanings, as demonstrated in media representations of "Black" athletes. An illustration of how bodies are read and racialized is clearly shown by James (2005) and the story of how his son was approached by a high-school basketball coach. His son's body was read as young, tall, "Black," and male, and racialized as interested and skilled in basketball. It is this same process that reads "Asian" bodies as conforming to the model minority thesis and therefore excelling in math and science while being frail and meek in athletics (Nakamura 2009) and that leads to the interrogation of certain body types or to the question "What are you?" if one does not fit easily into a racial group. Ambiguous bodies serve to reinforce rather than dismantle socially constructed racial categories. As King-O'Riain's work on Japanese American beauty pageants shows, there is an expectation of what an "authentically" Japanese American beauty queen should look like, and mixed race competitors who do not fit into this narrow characterization are questioned and criticized. In her words, "race still has a cultural conceptual primacy and connection to the body and physical appearance that is difficult for people to undo" (King-O'Riain 2006, 2).

Based on the process of lodging a protest outlined in the eligibility rules, it is clear that reading and racializing bodies is a key way in which individuals are grouped and categorized, because teams must assess whether a player or line-up is of the appropriate "content." A secondary way that this categorization takes place is through identification of ethnicity through last name. For example,

Nick (April 2007) recalled one tournament where the starting line-up was announced. "So if your last name isn't Wong or Chan then you know they're not Chinese." Mark (27 years old, second and third generation, mixed race) also recalled how a number of players would claim to be Chinese, but "it's like 'Yo, your last name is Kim! Come on!?' (laughs)." In this instance, last name could confer racial but not always ethnic belonging. This is in contrast to mixed-race Japanese American beauty pageant competitors who purposely used Japanese middle names when competing (King-O'Riain 2006). Race and ethnicity were conflated, whereby racial belonging was claimed using an ethnic strategy. For the NACIVT though, this strategy of determining racial belonging via an ethnic strategy may not be available, for two reasons. First, in a sporting context, it is more common to use last names on team jerseys. Second, because of the gendered norms of how family name is conferred, for those mixed-race players whose last name is that of a "non-Chinese" or "non-Asian" father, the last name becomes another way in which ethnic and racial belonging becomes tenuous. The techniques for claiming membership used by the mixed-race Japanese American beauty pageant contestants, therefore, may not be applicable in other settings and where there are different racial meanings in play.

During the NACIVT, the practice of reading and racializing bodies into distinct, albeit constructed, categories occurred mainly in terms of distinguishing those who are viewed as "100 per cent" or "full" from those who are "half" or "mixed" and those who are "not Asian."[1] The assumption of being able to read and identify someone as "Asian" operated as an informal boundary, prior to the codification of the eligibility rule. According to one interviewee who had been involved since the 1970s, "As long as you look[ed] Oriental, it's good," and teams "never check[ed] the background" of other players. This assumption of being able to identify easily who is "Asian" maintains the boundaries of membership because only those who are read as "Asian" are approached and recruited

---

1 In this situation, "mixed" did not include those who were of mixed Asian backgrounds, such as Korean and Japanese.

to participate. Furthermore, this knowledge and practice were viewed as common sense. During the Washington tournament, a player was answering questions from a spectator about the tournament. The player stated that "Asian" was determined "by blood," an explanation that was not questioned by the spectator. Adam (38 years old, first generation) described one US player as "look[ing] more White, but you could tell that he had *Asian blood in him*" (emphasis added). Similarly, as one player stated, "well you can *tell* they're Asian" (Field Notes, Washington Tournament, 3 September 2006). Recruiting based on the assumption of being able to read bodies accurately was one form of gatekeeping observed by Chin (2012) in her study on Japanese American basketball leagues. The category of "Asian" remained steadfastly real and tangible. Even when I asked them to specify how they knew someone was "Asian," the interviewees had trouble answering or could not provide an answer at all.

Because "Asianness" was perceived to be easily determined and due to the blood-quantum logic, even when thought to be "in there somewhere," players questioned the identities of "mixed-race Asian" participants who were read as more Other than "Asian." During the Washington tournament, for example, I heard an observer proclaim that "some of these guys look as White as me." If questioned, players had to provide evidence of their claims. This dubious standing could pose a problem for teams. Nick described how a recent addition to his club was "as White as that cooler [pointing to the white water cooler] with curly hair, but he had the papers to show that he was Chinese. I don't know how I'm going to say that this guy is Chinese." Nancy (28 years old, second generation) admitted that "sometimes you'll see some people who are coloured [sic] and you're like where's the Asian in you?" Being sceptical of Asian background was more pervasive when players were particularly talented. Tom, for example, remembered going to a tournament and playing against an athlete who he believed was Samoan and "everyone's like 'Come on!?!' […] I think he had a like five-foot vertical, it was just amazing, ridiculous." When I asked him if teams challenged the legality of this player's participation, he could not recall. Instead, he said that this scepticism was voiced during "pub talk, after the playing day, having a beer and going, 'Come on, that guy is *not* half! Gimme a break!?'" Another person spoke with confidence and authority that a certain player was *not* Asian, even if this individual had an affidavit stating otherwise.

While these examples remained at the level of gossip, Adam described how teams were told that players whose "Asian" background was disavowed had to be removed from their roster:

> I remember a case with a girl's team [...] She was supposedly mixed, Black and Chinese, but she looked more Black, or not Chinese, Black and Asian, I can't remember whether she was Chinese or not but she looked more Black than she was Asian so one of the organizing cities didn't let her play because of that.
>
> I remember a story and I remember seeing the guy, too. He was a, he looked Indian-ish, Southeast Indian kind of thing. *Really* good player [...] But one tournament, he played in and he basically, he destroyed, he killed every team that he played against. The next Labour Day tournament, the tournament committee got in contact with the [...] team and said you cannot put this guy on your roster, he is not Chinese.

Based on the racial arithmetic of two equal parts making a whole, Adam's claim that the player "looked more Black than she was Asian" made him and members of an organizing committee sceptical of the player's "supposed" mixed background. Clearly, the reading of these two individuals relies on fixed notions of what features count as "Black" or "Indian-ish," and on the presumed accuracy of how these markers are read. Furthermore, their lack of racial belonging is used as evidence of their lack of ethnic belonging.

Unlike the accepted obviousness of "Asianness," there were some forms of difference that remained invisible. Amber acknowledged that "people lie sometimes and they'll write down [on the roster] that they're 100 per cent, but they're only like half, they're like half-Chinese and half-Vietnamese, but that seems to like slip by because you really can't prove or you really can't tell." In other words, racial purity could be conferred despite a mixed ethnic background because the differences among Asians were seen as indistinguishable. In another example, one male interviewee who is not Chinese admitted that he wore the jersey of a Chinese teammate so that he could continue playing without having the team accused of fielding an illegal line-up. According to this player, "no one would call it because they can't see it, they can't see the visual difference. So therefore, it's kinda tough to call." The "visual difference" to which this interviewee refers is the difference that "50 per cent Asian" players presumably possess but multi-ethnic "100 per cent Asian" players do not. This invisibility posed a problem for one senior player from the United States, because if players "look Asian, then it's difficult to tell" whether they are Chinese or not and to determine whether opposing teams are abiding by the two-thirds rule. Thus, ethnicity became invisible when bodies were being read and racialized via the lens of Asianness.

These examples, particularly that of the senior player from the United States who deemed it problematic that an "Asian" player could pass as a "Chinese" player, highlight the tension between racial and ethnic belonging within the NACIVT. Whereas elsewhere ethnic competency could serve as evidence of racial belonging (e.g., King-O'Riain 2006), in the NACIVT, racial belonging can actually pose a risk to the surety of ethnic community. There is a risk of diluting ethnicity, particularly Chineseness, when identifying with a broader racial category of Asian. We can see parallels with the early years of the Asian American movement, where the greater influence of Japanese, West Coast, heterosexual, male voices resulted in the subsequent silencing of Other Asian voices (e.g., queer, women, working class, and so on) (see also Thangaraj 2015a, 2015b for discussion of South Asian American community). While banding together under the banner of Asian American provided a stronger political platform, it also risked adding to the homogenizing imperative of viewing Asian American as a uniform entity. Expanding the boundaries of belonging to allow participation in the NACIVT to include Asianness renders Chinese ethnicity less visible.

Based on these examples, it is clear that two boundaries are being policed through the reading and racializing of bodies. The first boundary is that of "Asian" and "not Asian," since only those athletes who were read as "Asian" or "even remotely Asian, they'll come find you" (Leo). The second boundary was between "100 per cent Asian" and those who were not, whereby participants who were viewed as "half" were placed under additional scrutiny. Whereas the first reading took place outside of the tournaments, the second analysis of players' bodies occurred during tournaments, particularly the annual Labour Day Tournament, which was seen as more important than other competitions. This examination operated in terms of whether a line-up of an opposing team followed eligibility rules (i.e., that there were not more than one-third "non-100 per cent" Chinese players) and also at the level of questioning "Asian" background if players were of mixed race. As Helen (34 years old, second generation) put it, "You're always looking like, 'Oh, is that person Chinese? Are they Chinese? Are they cheating?'"

The marking of boundaries through the reading and racializing of players creates a hierarchy of bodies (see figure 2.1). For example, Christie (25 years old, second generation) stated that "being full Chinese is like the best thing," although she quickly added that other people are not upset with the "full Chinese" players. She explained how this hierarchy affects individuals who are not "full Chinese" in terms of the line-up: "Even if you're a better player or you're tied with someone who is of full Chinese descent, that full Chinese person will get more play time." Sarah felt that as a "100 per cent Chinese" person,

> there's already a spot that I can take [...]. I can help to come in and play defence and I can help with the legality issues [i.e., eligibility rule issues]. So in that sense I feel like, sometimes, there's a little extra, like if you were really good and you're full, you have that much more of an advantage.

Skill level is certainly important; however, being "100 per cent Chinese" did provide an "advantage." Irene (26 years old, second generation), who admits that she is not a high-calibre player, had to deal with the lack of playing time on many occasions, even getting little to no playing time despite travelling far for tournaments.

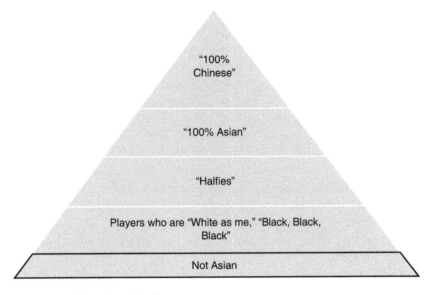

Figure 2.1 Hierarchy of bodies.

She said cynically that "if I was Chinese, [my experience] would be a little bit different (laughs)." Despite Christie's assertion that "non-Chinese Asian" players did not feel resentment, the fact that they are referred to as illegals, "foreign" (Brian), and so on, and that some refer to themselves as "illegit," suggests otherwise. Even "full Chinese" players may be conscious of this hierarchy and their "special status." Nancy, for example, described herself as being *"fortunate* to be 100 per cent Chinese" (emphasis added). Even a highly exceptional player, one who was heavily recruited by an NACIVT team in Toronto and who has also found success outside of the NACIVT, is described in Liang's (2014) documentary film as having one "thing going against him; he's half." Thus, despite his remarkable volleyball skills, his position within the hierarchy is fixed.

At the bottom of this hierarchy are those who are deemed "not Asian" by the eligibility rules. Those players who are read as not possibly having any "Asian" background, such as the player who is as "White as the water cooler," "White as me," or "Black, Black, Black" (Karen), may also be rendered as "not Asian," and therefore seen not to belong. In some cases, these individuals stand as evidence of a decline in upholding the rules: before, "they used to be strict about it, but now it's gone the other way" (a spectator, Field Notes, Washington Tournament). This hierarchy is not stable, however, as individuals have moved between categories, such as the player who wore the jersey of a Chinese teammate, players whose last name can be mistaken for a Chinese one, or players whose physical appearance may be read as putting them in the "half-Asian" category.

This hierarchizing or relational positioning (Brah, 1996) of players illustrates how groups can be represented as similar or different and subsequently included or excluded. As Brah indicates, where several diasporas intersect – in this case various trajectories of Asian diasporas – these groups can be constructed vis-à-vis one another. Furthermore, different transnational histories can have implications for interrelationships, giving an example of the entangled trajectories of the Chinese and Japanese diasporas. Although in this study such tensions did not emerge, the positioning of "100 per cent Chinese" and mixed race, multi-ethnic "Chinese" and "Asian" categories illustrates the multi-axial positioning of groups in relation to one another within diaspora (Brah 1996).

Through examining the relationship with Others and with difference and identifying the contours of diaspora, we can see that the NACIVT community is grounded in ideas of "race." There are layers of belonging within this community, with the outermost boundary being that of "Asian," a category determined by biological race because individuals must conform to the socially constructed phenotype of Asianness, one that does not include South Asianness. This Asianness is presumed to be innate and obvious, reflected by bloodlines, proven by physicality, and measurable via blood-quantum rules. Asianness could be read on the bodies of players, allowing players to racialize and assign people to distinct, albeit constructed, categories, a process and result that were viewed as routine and common sense. Perhaps in part because I was read as a "fellow-Asian," interviewees would often presume that I *obviously* could tell the difference between Asians and non-Asians and between "100 per cent" and "mixed" and also could tell whether there is "Asian in there somewhere." Admittedly, I would catch myself engaging in this practice during the participant observation of the tournaments.

Asianness, though, despite the assumption of continuity and recognizable uniformity, subsumes different ethnicities, which are reflected in who counts as "Asian" in the eligibility rules. Race continues to overdetermine "Asian," though nation-state and country of origin are used as stand-in criteria. Subsequent layers of belonging are more explicitly determined by blood-quantum rules, with mixed-race Chinese and mixed-race Asian players being situated lower in the hierarchy of players. Furthermore, mixed-race individuals are unable to claim ethnic or racial belonging because of their biology, which is in turn equated with their lack of ethnicity membership. The fact that these notions and equations circulate among the participants, and that they are generally accepted as fact and as justification for how boundaries are defined, demonstrates how assumptions about primordial identity can hold fast and stick (e.g., King-O'Riain 2006). Nonetheless, the boundaries identified and the connections made to the body and physicality are continually being remade in response to conflicts when people have crossed "the line" (Jeffery Chung, quoted in Liang 2014).

Enforcing Boundaries

Although interviewees rely on primordial definitions of Asianness, they still engage in an ongoing process of producing this collectivity, in large part because of the conflicts and challenges that have arisen as a result of the eligibility rules, the very things that establish the boundaries of membership within the NACIVT community. As Brah (1996) states, in using diaspora as a concept, it is imperative to examine how it is produced and how individuals negotiate social divisions. The participants' responses and reactions to the eligibility rules, the boundaries the rules demarcate, and instances of rule-breaking (or boundary-crossing) illustrate the limits of collective identity and the imperfect fit between an identity category and the lived experience of that category (Ang 2001). Indeed, the diversity of reactions to perceived rule breaches illustrates the contradictory and hybrid experience of membership within the NACIVT specifically and of diaspora generally.

Reactions to violations of the eligibility rules were unique to the NACIVT because it is a sports setting: responses were dependent on the skill level of the players in question. Most interviewees agreed that if the team was of mediocre calibre and unlikely to advance to higher rounds of competition, then violations of the eligibility rules would not be punished and the boundary between "Asian"/"non-Asian" would not be reviewed. One interviewee admitted that his status was never questioned because his team was not considered a threat to other teams vying to advance to the final rounds. When players suspected teams of having individuals of dubious "Asian" status, their suspicions would be voiced to one another during post-game socials, such as Tom's recollection of gossiping about a particularly talented player. This discussion of questionable players might also take place over the Internet, using website message boards. For example, in the previous nacivt.com website, after the completion of one Labour Day tournament, a user asked for information about the results for the men's finals. An individual known as "T Dot Rules" responded that a Toronto team had won, despite the fact that the opposing team was "stacked up" with three strong players, listing their names. The user responded "What?!?! [Smith] was allowed to play?!?!" (*NACIVT.com guestbook* n.d.; response dated 8 September 2005). Later, when I shared this story with a former player who had been involved in the NACIVT for several years, she explained why there was such a surprised and incredulous reaction to Smith's participation. She explained that Smith does not have an "Asian" background, as outlined in the rules, and so should not have been playing.

When teams were closer to advancing to the finals and felt that another team was not abiding by the eligibility rules, they could issue a protest. As Nick puts it, "The rule is such that, as long as you're the bottom dwellers, not getting to the playoffs and so on, nobody cares. But as soon as you get to the upper echelon, 'Oh, let's get that rule out and see whether we can take a few guys off the team!'" This point was reiterated by other players, like Adam, who said that "If you feel that *that* team that you're going to be playing with, that you think does not have the proper content, if they're really good, you better call them out." Nancy also stated that if the team was not good, then breaking the rules "makes no difference, might as well let them play." Boundaries then became much more pertinent when the question of winning or losing and potentially advancing to the next round was at stake. Furthermore, since the rules were being enforced to garner an advantage over a potentially stronger team, how these rules are lived and experienced is inextricably tied to ideas of the "strength" and "advantage" of "impure blood" and/or taller/faster/stronger genes (chapter 3).

The process for issuing a challenge is discussed during the Captain's Meeting the evening before the start of the tournament. For the Washington tournament in 2006, every captain was given a handout outlining the protest process. There are three types of protests that can be issued: Type A. Individual Player Eligibility; Type B. Lineup Legality; and Type C. Work Team. Type A and B protests have implications for the boundary of "Asian/non-Asian," and "100 per cent" or "full" and "half." In either case, only a team captain may approach the head referee. If a player's "Asian" background is in question, then the protest must occur once the "individual under speculation" has set foot on the court during a match (Protest process handout, Washington 2006 tournament). Once the protest has been made, the game is stopped, and the target of the protest is identified. Should the captain of "the accused" team concede that the participant is not of "Asian" descent, the player must leave the court and is not permitted to participate in any matches for the rest of the tournament. Should the captain wish to defend the player, then the head referee, the captains from both teams, and the individual in question must report to the control centre of the tournament. Photo identification of the player is then provided and eligibility is verified by comparing the identification to the official team roster.

The legality of a line-up may be challenged at any point during a game. A captain can issue a protest upon suspicion that the opposing team has a line-up in which more than one-third of the players are not "100 per cent Chinese," at which point the opposing captain may concede and make appropriate changes to the line-up. If the captain refuses to make these modifications, all players must remain on the court while a second referee retrieves the accused team's roster from the control centre. The head referee then confirms the on-court players by asking for their names and verifying their eligibility using the official roster. If the accused team is found to be in violation, the line-up must be changed. While not indicated in the 2006 DC NACIVT Protest Process, interviewees mentioned that any points obtained by the team while in violation are deducted. In addition to this penalty, it was considered very embarrassing for a team to be caught cheating. Nancy recalled how a coach was found trying to "sneak in ... aliens or ... non-content" players. She speculated that this coach never attempted this again "because it's embarrassing you know that you're trying to [cheat] and in the end it's all about honesty." This shame both helped to ensure that this coach and others adhered to the rules and indirectly reproduced the boundaries of "legal" and "illegal" and, ultimately, of "full," "Asian," "non-Asian," and so on.

Despite the codified rules and formalized process for issuing a protest against teams that did not abide by them, a number of respondents stated that to issue a protest was considered bad form or "a little bit of more of a hostile move" (Diane). Teams that issued protests or "called out" opposing teams were viewed as "a bunch of sucks" (Hugh) and poor sports. Even when a player is known to be not of the ethnicity that he or she is claiming, Hugh stated that his team would not issue a protest. This view does not appear to have changed. Phoebe (22 years old, second generation), whom I interviewed in 2015, recalled a protest that was issued against her team and said "the team that called us out doesn't have the greatest rep right now." These negative perceptions may be in part because of the presumed motivation that protests were being made in order to limit the strength of a particular team or to gain an advantage.

As Tom notes, only if the player "was a really really good player then it'd be challenged in the tournament." The negative view of teams that used the eligibility rules against an opponent also stemmed from a perception of hypocrisy. For example, Mark was critical of those individuals who strongly advocated that opposing teams adhere to the rules but were themselves "fielding teams that are half illegitimate line-ups." In light of the negative perception of teams, one would hesitate before issuing a protest, because "You don't really wanna be the *bad* person by saying you can't play because you're not Chinese or you don't fall into that [category]" (Adam). In fact, one player, who recalled issuing a protest, repeatedly explained to me that his team protested *only* because "another team told us they were going to call [this team] out if they play them so I knew they were going to do that. So we did it first." It was clear that I was to understand that the other team's intention justified his team's protest. This view of teams that issue challenges may have changed since the time of these initial interviews, however, as subsequent interviewees (2015) were adamant that protests happen regularly and frequently at the Labour Day tournaments.

Moments of Inclusion

Although diaspora's Others have been kept at bay for the most part, there were some examples of inclusion (albeit contested) that signal subtle changes that are occurring with regard to who is included and who has legitimate status within the NACIVT. Even with the salient threat of White athleticism, a few interviewees noted that there had been cases of White players participating in the NACIVT, with one elder dismissing the significance of their participation, claiming that one player could not change the course of a game. Nevertheless, given the increasing presence of mixed-race Asian athletes, coupled with the anxiety linked to White athleticism, the construction of White as a threat to this diaspora is still pervasive. Indeed, the fact that there is a White player who has allegedly lied about having Asian ancestry and has chosen to dye his/her hair to further diminish his/her whiteness illustrates this binary. Similarly, the fact that a woman has served as a setter on a nine-man team illustrates how gender hierarchies may be resisted and points to new ways of imagining what nine-*player* volleyball could look like. Having said that, though, such a move would do little to address the relative lack of status of the women's game and of women athletes in general (see chapter 3).

There are additional instances of inclusion, such as the crossing of class lines. For example, in the official history, volleyball "broke down barriers of [...] class between laundry workers and privileged students" ("A short history" 1999, 24). Decades later, Eli (26 years old, second generation, mixed race) reiterated how volleyball served as an opportunity to bring people of diverse backgrounds together. His team consisted of people "from all different professions, students, high school students, factory workers to physiotherapists, myself a [skilled professional], computer programmers, engineers, we even have a surgeon on our alumni team."

The inclusion of people of varying ages was also observed on one Washington team that had an adolescent boy in his early teens on the same team as someone in his late fifties. Steve (31 years old, second generation) also said with pride that there is no age limit in the NACIVT, allowing for adolescents to enter the tournament and for older players to remain involved for many years. Furthermore, he explained that there is "no calibre segregation" in that teams are not assigned to different pools based on ability, and even beginners can compete in the tournament. In the nines game, in particular, mediocre players can still participate, although those who are less skilled or are new to the game may be assigned to back-row positions. Shorter individuals may also be placed in the back row. Players who are less proficient in particular skills are still effective within nines volleyball because there is no rotation, making it unnecessary to excel in all positions and allowing for specializing in certain skills. Thus, this version of volleyball, some interviewees argued, is more inclusive of people of a range of playing abilities. While this may be true, they are not accounting for people who may have diverse mobility needs and who would be excluded from the game on that account. Furthermore, with the increasing competitiveness of the tournament, teams are becoming more and more discriminating as to which players will be chosen to start or even get court time during the course of the tournament, making it difficult to maintain the view that the tournament is an inclusive event. Nevertheless, it is important to acknowledge the different moments of inclusion – whether in terms of gender, class, age, or ability – that were observed and lauded by interviewees. While these moments may still offer little comfort to those who are excluded by the eligibility rules, they do make plain that rules and boundaries can be crossed.

Crossing Boundaries

While the view of teams that issue a protest may have changed over time, what has not changed is that the eligibility rules have often been disregarded. Adam recalled, for instance, that his team always hoped that they would not get caught, despite the "many times that we would have. We were breaking the content rule, but *all teams do it*" (emphasis added). Furthermore, Mark insisted that protests occur at every tournament. He was not alone in this view, which suggests that these boundaries are crossed on a regular basis. One particular coach was known to ignore the rules and would put on the strongest possible line-up until the team was caught. A former player from another club recounted how his team deliberately used a "non-Asian" player on the roster with forged documents that claimed Chinese status. Apparently, the birth certificate of a former player who was not attending the tournament was used.

Interviewees who were not "Chinese" also recalled being part of strategies to disregard the rules. The example of the player who switched jerseys with a Chinese teammate has already been noted. In this instance, he did this of his own accord and not because of his coach's instructions. On another occasion, though, he was written in the official roster as Chinese because his last name is a common Chinese last name. In fact, when he was first recruited by the coach and senior members of his current club, upon realizing that he was not Chinese, they asked if he knew any active NACIVT players and whether they were aware of his ethnic background. They also said that "they would pass me off as Chinese." The player did not seem to mind this negation of his own ethnic identity. Rather, he preferred it because "then I can play as much as I want and not have to worry about it." Another "non-Chinese" player recalled that her teammates and coach would often discuss the possibility of putting her on as a starter, even though this would put them over the one-third limit. She admitted that a few times she was a starter on her team or would be called to substitute for another player, resulting in an illegal line-up. Her ethnicity on the official roster was never given as Chinese, but the coach would occasionally simply put her on, and take a wait-and-see approach.

James, a coach, also disregarded the rule because he did not want to discourage people from participating. His motive for ignoring the rule was not explicitly a desire to win but the result of experiences in other leagues of being told that he would not be able to play because of similar eligibility rules despite being a strong player. Thus, James "loosely adopt[ed] or at least conform[ed] to the idea that it's a Chinese tournament." He asked rhetorically, "Is it really wrong if nobody ever asks you? Like if nobody is going to protest you, wait until they protest and then make it in an issue." Thus, he places the onus on his opponents. Opposing teams may decline to enforce the rules, however, even when they know of non-eligible players. Just as Hugh refused to protest teams, even when he was aware of an infraction, Carol stated that she has "never looked at the opposing team for non-Chinese" players. The rules and therefore definitions of membership could be ignored both by players or coaches who broke the rules and by those who refused to enforce them.

Unlike those who disregarded the rules, some players felt ambivalent and seemed to be unsure about the eligibility rules. They had difficulty articulating their feelings about the regulations or expressed contradictory views. Owen (48 years old, second generation), for example, at first insisted that "it doesn't make a difference, I just like to play, whether they're Chinese or not. It doesn't really matter to me." Here he emphasized his participation in the game and that his involvement was not impacted by whether other players were "Chinese" or not. He then later seemed to hint at the importance of the rules in ensuring fairness and acknowledged that he would prefer a team to be legal. This was then followed by an admission that his own team had not followed the content rule during the past few years. Thus, it was clear that it does not matter with whom he plays *on his own team*, since his team has not been able to follow the requirements of the eligibility rule. His particular club has a long history in the NACIVT and had won the championship in its early days. However, it had not seen that level of success for a few decades. In some years, the men's team in his club even had difficulty fielding a team, a challenge faced by some clubs in the NACIVT over the years. Within such a context where there are not enough players or where there is a desire to recapture the former glory of the club, coaches may field an illegal line-up out of desperation to form any team, or a competitive team, while still wanting the other team to play fair.

Ultimately, Owen states that, "if the rule's there, people should abide by it – I guess that's what I should say (laughs)." The simultaneous indifference and recognition of the importance of fairness and following rules illustrate the ambivalent feelings he has towards the eligibility rules. That he finished with what he thinks he *should* say about the eligibility rules is further indication of this ambivalence, as well as the inability to reconcile the view that sport is apolitical and upholds ideas like merit, abiding by rules, and so on, and the reality that sport is far from neutral and is a site where boundaries, be they of gender, sex, race, or ethnicity, are negotiated.

Critiquing Boundaries

Mixed feelings towards the rule were also expressed in terms of the impact on players. For example, Steve recalled when one of the teams in his club was caught using an illegal line-up. As a result, the roster of starting players had to be changed, "and it disappointed the guys who were starters but were not allowed to play because they were Korean or half-Chinese. And I felt bad for them, because they trained all summer and they came to compete" but now could not play in the positions they had earned. Steve had never experienced this, since he was "100 per cent Chinese." However, he could empathize with these other players and the frustration they felt. Perhaps Rachel's comment regarding the rules best exemplifies this ambivalence: "I don't know all the rules, and sometimes I hear about them and I'm just ... I don't know who enforces them or who decides, but sometimes I think it's really ... random. How do you decide?"

Rachel's telling observation of the seemingly "random" nature of the rules also reflects participants' criticism of the rules. Just as she asks, "How do you decide?," interviewees critiqued the ways in which "Chinese" and "Asian" were defined. For example, James stated that he disagreed with the rules that dictated that someone who was "one-quarter" or "one-eighth Chinese" would not be permitted to play "because your ethnicity isn't Chinese enough." Although no such rule exists, James's comment reflects the practice of reading bodies to determine whether they sufficiently exhibit racialized features of "Chineseness" (and "Asianness") and the need to provide evidence of one's ethnicity. Rob's comments were similarly critical of how "Asian" was defined in arbitrary ways:

> Asian was defined how? It was East Asian because we get into, well, is Indian Asian? And then all the reactionary response, "Well, no," you know? But it's "No, no, no, we mean Japanese and Korean." Oh, so you mean Northeast. What about Vietnamese?" "Okay, okay, maybe Vietnamese." So you got this kind of stuff right?

Likewise, Irene wondered "Where do you draw the line between who's Asian and who's not? Does South Asian count if you're Indian? Can you play? I don't know." Whereas one of the elders had little difficulty defining for me the acceptable region as "basically Asia Pacific," Irene questioned how these boundaries were being demarcated.

Interviewees also pointed out how "Chineseness" was being defined and proven in seemingly concrete but in fact tenuous ways. Steve explained that "Chineseness" could be proven by showing a passport, or other identification that provides one's full name. He admitted, however, that it would be difficult to distinguish whether someone with the last name "Lee," for instance, is Chinese or Korean. Graham also observed that Vietnamese last names may be mistaken for Chinese surnames (September 2007). Using forms of identification like passports to confirm that a player has a Chinese last name illustrates the ambiguity of who and what counts as Chinese. Last name and ancestry become linked, as it is presumed that an ethnic Chinese last name would be passed down from one generation to the next. Thus, the name becomes symbolic of a connection "back" to the homeland of China. In this case, "Chinese" identity is defined as originating from China (Tu 1991), and "Chineseness" is treated in essentialist and absolute ways because it mandates deference to "original tradition" in order to be considered "authentic" (Ang 2001). The implications of such positioning are discussed by Lowe (1996) and illuminated by Ang's personal account of telling someone that she does not speak Chinese[2] and being told that she was a "fake Chinese" because she did not fit into the specific category into which she had been placed. Her inability to speak Chinese was "hegemonically constructed as a lack, a sign of loss of authenticity" (Ang 2001, 30). On the other hand, Rob's teammate, who could trace his origins to China, experienced the limits of his "authenticity" and the arbitrariness of "Chinese" thusly defined. This player who was of mixed Chinese and Latin American background, "grew up in Toisan, spoke Toisanese perfectly. How can anyone not call him Chinese?" Being raised in China and speaking Toisanese fluently were markers of "Chinese" identity, and yet this player was not included within the category of "Chineseness."

---

2 Meaning any one of the various languages spoken in China.

This example also illuminates the categorization of mixed race "Chinese" players. Specifically, many interviewees felt that it was unfair that players who had only one "Chinese" parent were not considered "Chinese." Steve stated that

> there's a lot of interracial marriages these days, so a kid who's half-Scottish and half-Chinese, are you trying to tell me that he or she is not Chinese? Well they *are* Chinese and now we're making them not Chinese [according to the eligibility rules].

Similarly, Adam felt that it was unjust that, when applied to children of mixed "Chinese" background, "all of a sudden that Chinese in them no longer counts." Karen recalled the frustrations of one of her teammates who was "half-Chinese" but identified more with her Chinese heritage:

> She just really felt like, you know how are they defining this ethnic line and if it's really a Chinese rule, then why is it that I don't get to play as much as a full Chinese person when I feel ethnically I am more Chinese?

Implicit in the rule, these critiques, and the frustration expressed by Karen's teammate is that "pure" Chineseness is the only Chineseness of value.

Similarly, John (21 years old, second generation) observed that he knew some players who were "half-Chinese" and they could

> speak better Chinese than some of the full Chinese players. [...] They're more immersed in the culture than people that are of full Chinese descent that have grown up in Canada. So if [NACIVT] is a cultural thing, then that person [who speaks Chinese] is more cultured ... what gives them the right to not be considered full Chinese?

Here, "Chineseness" was defined in terms of demonstrating "authentic" markers of "Chineseness," as well as the culturalist notion of feeling that one has Chinese cultural heritage (Ang 2001). These ways of understanding "Chineseness" illustrate how some individuals would not "count" as Chinese and yet would still think of themselves as such. John's rationale that some of his teammates were more Chinese than "some of the full Chinese players" parallels the example of mixed-race beauty pageant contestants who would claim ethnic belonging through exhibiting cultural markers of ethnicity (King-O'Riain 2002), in this case language proficiency. Although this critique attempts to "rescue" the assertion of "Chineseness," especially evident in how Karen and John speak of the unfair treatment of their teammates, Ang (2001) states that this view of "Chineseness" can perpetuate the struggle for "authentic" culture and can reinforce feelings of guilt or incompetence. Nevertheless, these examples show that the interviewees questioned how the rules were grounded in definitions of "Chineseness" that valued only "pure" Chinese and subsequently dismissed the Chinese heritage of players who were of mixed background.

Although the study participants felt it unfair to discount the claim to "Chineseness" for players who are "half," many of the interviewees were hesitant to go as far as calling the rules racist. Rob was one of the few who was quick to state that "it all smacks of racism," while others, like Peter, who described it as a "dilemma," struggled with the issue of racism. This uncertainty may be in part because individuals were unclear what counted as racism. Nancy rhetorically asked, "Is it discriminating against other cultures? I don't know. Maybe ... maybe it isn't." Sandy (35 years old, first generation) also waffled back and forth between rejecting and agreeing with accusations of racism. She said that "if you want to call an exclusivity racism, then I guess you can call it and label it that." Other interviewees called the NACIVT racist volleyball with varying degrees of conviction. Amber for example, said that a number of her teammates call it "racist volleyball because it is somewhat racist, even towards other Asians," while another interviewee stated that other players label their photos related to NACIVT on their personal websites "Racist Volleyball" as a joke, implying that this practice of naming the NACIVT racist was less (or not just) a statement of judgment and perhaps more an example of mockery.

While there may be hesitation to explicitly and seriously call the eligibility rules racist, a number of interviewees felt that the eligibility rules were dated and needed to be revised, especially in light of changing demographics. For example, Peter, Lisa, Steve, and John all pointed out that interracial and interethnic marriages are increasing in number and that "no one's just going to stick to their own race" (John). Likewise, Nick gave transformations in the population as reason for a modification of the rules; however, he specifically referred to the increasingly diverse Chinatowns in both Canada and the United States, which, he observed, were no longer the domain of "Chinese" people but home to a variety of "Asian" people. Two players from Canada also argued that for the NACIVT to disregard interracial marriage was a barrier to promoting multiculturalism because such a position was premised on the notion that cultures should not mix. Thus, the rules needed to reflect and be sensitive to these changes. Their reference to multiculturalism may have been a result of their Canadian context. Christie, in particular, highlighted the contradiction of the NACIVT in that it offered a way to preserve culture, which is aligned with multiculturalism, and yet the NACIVT failed to promote unity and inclusiveness by excluding and limiting the opportunities of some people.

Some suggestions included "giv[ing] full credentials" (John) to players with one parent or grandparent who is "Chinese," rather than relegating them to the "Other" category. Interviewees also thought that the proportions of "100 per cent Chinese" and "non-Chinese Asians" allowed should be changed from the current two-thirds to half, so that only half of the players were required to be "full Chinese." Christie hoped that the grandfather clause would be amended so that each year players who had participated for a total of ten years could have the eligibility rules waived and be considered "full Chinese." Peter (36 years old, first generation) anticipated that in future the mandatory minimum number of "Chinese" players on the court would also be removed. A number of interviewees felt that it should be open to all "Asian" groups, often using the language of bloodline as to how membership would be determined (i.e., if you have Asian blood, then you can play).

Notwithstanding these suggestions for change expressed by some of the interviewees, I only came across two instances where such questioning of boundaries has become a formal discussion item on the agenda for the pre-Labour Day tournament Captain's Meeting. Despite the frequency with which this issue is apparently raised, in the almost three decades since the rules were codified, no substantial changes have been made. For example, one respondent suggested that the rules be changed to allow "non-Asian" players to constitute one-third of the line-up in order to reduce ambiguity (although the problem of definitions would still remain – e.g., to which category would a "one-quarter Asian" person be assigned?). This suggestion was not taken up. In another instance, Karen recounted a request made in the early 2000s by a mixed-race "Chinese" player who pushed to have "half-Chinese" players be recognized as "full Chinese" in order to differentiate them from players who do not have Chinese "origins." According to Karen, the player wrote a letter that was presented to the tournament organizers and captains. The proposal was quickly rejected for reasons unknown at the time, and the player did not receive any formal feedback.

When Karen first shared this information with me, I was unable to interview this player, even with an introduction from Karen. This was in part because of geographical distance but also because of how difficult the player had found the experience; I learned of this almost a decade later when I finally had an opportunity to interview this individual. Admittedly, because of the years that had passed since her time with the NACIVT, this former player's memory was hazy. She did remember writing the letter and that "nothing happened" or came from her actions. In retrospect, she contextualized her actions within a lifelong pattern of having her claim to "Chineseness" questioned or denied, and within a period in her life when she was going through considerable emotional upheaval and change as she transitioned from one life stage into another. The issues that were being raised within a broader context, such as the general anti-Asian sentiment resulting from the arrival of migrants and asylum seekers from China to Canadian shores in 1999 and the subsequent hysteria about illegal migrants and "inv-Asians" (Fleras 2011, 139), did not specifically inform her decision to call for change.

According to this interviewee, the rejection of her petition for full recognition of "half-Chinese" players was complicated by gender and generational conflicts. Specifically, she felt that her teammates were seen as "confrontational, trouble-making kind of girls" and that they were not what the older generation of players in the club "were expecting in terms of subordinating and listening." She and her teammates "were always very respectful and obedient," but they nevertheless "spoke out and probably more tipped towards the feminism side." Further, she speculated that perhaps the older generation of players did not agree with her politics, and thus, "My voice wasn't necessarily welcome; my opinion may not have been welcomed and [was] seen as being like trying to stir things up" (see chapter 3 for detailed discussion of gender).

What is clear, even from her memory, is that the eligibility rules went beyond playing time. For this player, to be subject to the rules

> was very hurtful 'cause I do identify as being a Chinese person and I speak Chinese and Chinese is actually my first language, but I look very White and so for me to feel Chinese but to be treated like I wasn't Chinese enough was like a very, very difficult thing for me to be able to stay with the club.

Despite the camaraderie and strong bonds formed with her teammates, a number of whom remained her close friends almost two decades later, this player could not resolve the contradiction between feeling a sense of belonging and experiencing rejection as a result of being mixed race.

Among individuals who were directly affected by the eligibility rules, many subsequently experienced disunity in unity (Clifford 1997) as they tried to reconcile a meaningful sense of belonging with the frequent experience of being marginalized and dismissed. After interviewing players who were affected by the eligibility rules, I was left with a strong impression of their feelings of disappointment, resignation, uncertainty, and being devalued and defeated. This was poignantly expressed by Irene in particular.

Irene became involved in the NACIVT after moving to a new city. As a result of her participation, the team and the NACIVT community became her social network and provided a sense of belonging in a city that was new to her. While she greatly enjoyed participating in volleyball, the practices, and the tournaments, and was very loyal to her club, her experience had been mixed. She competed with other "non-Chinese" players for the position that she played and, being a newer player, did not have seniority. Added to this, she admitted that she was only a mid-level player. With all these factors combined, Irene saw very little court time during the tournaments.

During the interview, she recalled a tournament when she did not get to play very much, particularly near the end of the event when the possibility of advancing to the finals became a reality. Her sense of resignation was clear:

> How long can you really be satisfied with always sitting? [...] At the end of the day, you know. It's never going to be easy, and I think after a while you realize, well, practices are great, but when you spend a lot of money to go to a tournament, even if ... the money isn't really an issue, but if you spend all that money, you want to get something out of it in return too.

She explained that because she was not warned beforehand that she probably would not be playing, "you always have a hope. [...] If you don't want me to play, that's cool, but just tell me and then at least I know 'cause then I won't be thinking 'Maybe this time ...?'" Despite her insistence that she was fine with not playing so long as she was informed in advance, there was still an element of disappointment and pain reflected in her reference to the remote possibility and hope of playing.

Irene expressed feelings of doubt regarding her place and her role on the team, feelings that were highlighted if her coach did not play her. If she was not told beforehand that she might not get many opportunities to play, she would be confused as to why she did not get to participate. She described this experience as not "really know[ing] where [the coaches] wanted me." If she was warned prior to the game, "then at least I know where I stand." These feelings of uncertainty seemed to increase over time, as Irene realized that she was becoming one of the older players and seeing "a lot of younger people that are Chinese who can come up [to the first line] and because I'm [not Chinese], it['s] kinda like ... and even now I don't know what's gonna happen later down the road." Irene had noted earlier in the interview that she was not threatened by younger players who are "Chinese" and were being promoted from the second string. She was excited by the potential contribution that these players would make towards winning a championship. Nonetheless, her statement suggests that she was certainly conscious of their presence and of the ultimate limiting effect on her playing time that they represented. This sense of "at-risk status" compounded feelings of uncertainty. Her situation was magnified one summer when she realized that there were "four of us now," in reference to non-Chinese Asian players, which meant she was competing with four people for the two spots available to her.

During the follow-up telephone interview after a local tournament, Irene stated that she did not play at all and had begun to consider changing teams. In fact, she had been approached by a player from another team who had noticed Irene's limited playing time. Enticed by the possibility of greater playing opportunities, she watched this team during the local tournament, only to realize that there were a number of "mixed" players on the team, suggesting that her situation would change little. Ultimately, she remained uncertain about her future with the team and in the NACIVT.

Irene was not alone in her frustrations or her sense of insecurity. Karen recalled, for example, how upset she felt at one particular Labour Day tournament when she and many "Other" players received little playing time:

> The coach explained that part of it is because I'm playing this new position but part of it is because they aren't allowed to have more than two non-full Chinese players on the court at a time. And since we

already had, I think half of our team weren't full Chinese, so I mean that's half of the team sharing two positions. It was really frustrating.

This came to be a common experience as she remembered another tournament where she and two other teammates had a total of half a set of playing time over the course of three days. She described the experience as "terrible. [...] but by this time we were kinda used to getting shafted."

Not surprisingly, some interviewees felt less valued than other players. James, for example, recalled a time when his captain said, "Yeah, you're going to have to sit this game out because our line-up is a certain [ethnic make-up]." They didn't say it in so many words, but [implied] "you're not Chinese enough to play right now." James's speculation that his supposed "deficiency" was the reason for his lack of participation suggests a consciousness of his second-class status. Irene's experiences also imply an awareness of her position as a back-up player. She recalled a time when she contemplated not going to a tournament but was encouraged to attend by her coach. She knew that his motivation was "well, just in case something happens we have to have [Irene]." Thus, she was only a "just in case" player, who would be needed only if something happened to other (more valuable) players.

Ultimately, most interviewees whose participation was restricted could see the limits and the end point of their involvement in the NACIVT. While they expressed frustration with the rules, they felt resigned to accept the status quo. Brian, for example, in response to the unfairness of the rule, simply responded, "Yeah, that's the league (shrugs his shoulders slightly)." Karen, who was particularly vocal and passionate during the interview about the unfairness of the rule, admitted that she never considered pushing for change:

I didn't really feel like it was my role or my position to say, "Hey, let non-Chinese Asian players play more, let ... give us equal playing time" because that wasn't, I mean that's not what the league was about so I just kinda had to accept the way it was and hope that it would change eventually.

Near the end of her NACIVT career, Karen and her fellow "illegit" teammates were also "burnt out" and "tired" because they felt powerless to make changes. Thus, despite her frustration, she accepted the situation and could only hope that someday the rules would be changed. John also accepted the rules, although he thought they were "crazy" and "so racist," because he did not feel he had the power to change them. As the years passed, Karen and her teammates who were in similar circumstances came to feel that, while the rules were unfair, they had to abide by them. Not surprisingly, their NACIVT careers were shorter than the careers of their "100 per cent Chinese" teammates. Brian observed that "people have quit because the team had too many non-Chinese people and they didn't get a lot of playing time." Peter, a long-time coach, found that most players would endure the frustration for the first two years, "but after that, [because of the eligibility rules] they probably usually either quit or I have to let them go."

Clearly, the interviewees had varying opinions regarding the eligibility rules and the boundaries they enforce and, in turn, diverse views about identity, definitions, categories, and membership. I too felt ambivalent about the need to maintain the rules, especially the boundary between non-Asian and Asian. A large part of me agrees with continuing the exclusivity, despite the arbitrary and racialized way in which these lines are drawn. I too imagined how wonderful it would be for my children to participate in the tournament someday. With the event already at maximum capacity, opening it up for all to play would certainly diminish the chance to participate as the number of people who wish to play increases. Having said that, because I personally would fall into the "illegit/illegal/alien" category, I think it is unfair that the playing time of "100 per cent Chinese" players is protected at the expense of others. I have to admit that when I discovered that the rule came into being in 1991 and that the tradition of limiting the play of non-Chinese Asians was *not* a time-honoured one, I felt a certain amount of delight in knowing that I could debunk a myth, one that is often used as justification. Or, when I learned that a revered elder felt that half-Chinese and even one-quarter Chinese players *should* be considered Chinese and be allowed to play at any time,

I immediately wanted to share it with others. I imagined telling this to one interviewee in particular, who has been involved in the event for several years, is well respected, and has spoken of his desire to push for the recognition of players who are of mixed Chinese background, thinking it would help his campaign.

If not directly affected by the rules, many of the interviewees expressed empathy for their fellow teammates and could understand the shorter commitment to the NACIVT as well as the desire for change. Even as an outsider who has never played in the NACIVT and therefore has not experienced the belonging and sense of community that the interviewees enjoy and wish to protect, I too could understand the interviewees' frustration and sense of powerlessness because I too would be limited in my ability to participate because I am not "100 per cent" Chinese. A number of interviewees even expressed varying ways in which the rules could be modified in order to be more inclusive. Only one lone individual stated that, should cheating become rampant, the tournament should become all "Chinese." In general, though, the majority of interviewees seemed to agree that the tournament should remained closed to "non-Asian" players. This final frontier was justified in large part by drawing on biological essentialism and how it manifests in the social construction of race, gender, and culture within the NACIVT (see chapter 3).

Photo 2.1 Toronto Connex and Washington, DC, Slackers, 2013, Washington, DC. Connex player 19 engages in a metre ball middle attack while other Connex players form cover. DC Slackers players prepare to block. Credit: Rosanna U.

Photo 2.2 San Francisco West Coast and Washington, DC, CYC, 2009, Los Angeles. The West Coast player in the power position jumps for a high ball while his team forms cover. Four CYC team players formulate their block. Credit: Rosanna U.

Photo 2.3 Toronto Connex and an unidentified team, 2018, New York. The photo shows a right side attack by Connex player Number 6. Credit: Rosanna U.

Chapter 3

Essentialism: Race, Gender, and Culture

Race

I was very excited when I managed to secure an appointment with Rob. He was someone whom a number of veteran players and alumni had suggested I interview, both during my initial data collection and in follow-up interviews a decade later. They described him as someone who knew a great deal about the tournament, its history, and its inner workings. It was Rob who pointed out to me that the tournament continues to be influenced by the view that the tournament is for disenfranchised, impoverished working-class, first-generation immigrants who only have Labour Day as a day for leisure. Rob (39 years old, second generation) speculated that these working-class roots continue to influence how the tournament has been managed in recent decades. In our discussion of the eligibility rules, Rob made the following comment:

> I think a lot of people still who participate and run this tournament, they're still thinking the way the people who originally set up the tournament were thinking. Those people were all first-generation immigrants doing manual labour, disenfranchised, living hand to mouth, who only had Labour Day off as their entire, as their only holiday in their entire year. This was a tournament run by cooks, waiters, and chefs. Not even chefs. Cooks and waiters. It's still being run in some ways with that type of mentality.

The mentality of being disenfranchised is critical to the justification of the eligibility rules. Specifically, the exclusion resulting from the eligibility rules is often rationalized by speaking from a position of shared victimization or what Razack and Fellows (1998) have called a "race to innocence" (337).

This strategy of calling on a history of racial discrimination and the potential for future victimization is an approach that was deployed in the construction of Asian American panethnicity. According to Espiritu (1992), panethnicity is "a politico-cultural collectivity made up of peoples of several, hitherto distinct, tribal or national origins" (2). The shift from smaller forms of affiliation to this larger-scale organization is not linear; rather, it ebbs and flows, indicating that these allegiances are "multitiered, situational, and partly ascribed" (8). Panethnic groups are new and therefore cannot claim a primordial origin. Their sense of unity is "forged primarily through the symbolic reinterpretation of a group's common history" (9). Culture is thus treated as being in flux, and is discussed analytically rather than as a descriptor. Common culture is not thought of as an indication of panethnicity. While Espiritu's focus is panethnicity at the organizational level, she states that pan-Asian consciousness or panethnicity at the individual level is demonstrated by "self-identification, pan-Asian residential, friendship and marriage patterns, and membership in pan-Asian organizations" (15).

One of the first catalysts of panethnicity that Espiritu (1992) identifies is the sense of shared discrimination. During the post–World War Two era, Asian groups came to see that they had common problems and goals, particularly around barriers to employment. Such sentiments provided a sense of commonality among Asians. Pan-Asian organizations formed as a result of feeling excluded, alienated, and powerless because of the lack of their own structures. Furthermore, Okamoto (2006) suggests that "occupational segregation of Asian Americans encourages the formation of national pan-Asian organizations" (20). Another factor that mobilized panethnic identity was the realization that solidarity with other Asians led to greater political influence, including access to social service funding. The most effective impetus for

Asian panethnicity was anti-Asian violence that resulted in "defensive solidarities" (Espiritu 1992, 134) because of an understanding that hostilities that were directed at an Asian group would affect other Asians as well.

Solidarity against anti-Asian discrimination was evident among the respondents when discussing the eligibility rules by linking them to a history of victimization. Steve explained, for example, that when the NACIVT is accused of being racist, he tries "to remind them 'well the reason why we had to do it this way is because when we immigrated here, we couldn't get permits at the YMCA or local gym.'" Christie also pointed to past victimization and a sense of survival when explaining the rationale for the eligibility rules:

> We all take pride in that there's a reason why this is, we go back to the history and Asians not being able to join gyms and clubs and having to find a way to network with other friends across the nations and be proud of themselves.

Similarly, Sandy points out that one of the key features of the NACIVT, playing volleyball outside on the street, was a direct result of racism that prevented Chinese people from gaining access to mainstream sports facilities. She finds it "ironic" that they are then accused of racism for limiting participation. In learning of this past victimization, however, she believes that people will "get a better grasp and understanding and maybe even sympathy towards how this all started, then you might think it's less and less of a racist sport." The rationalizing of the eligibility rules that limit participation to Asian people by calling on a history of when Asian people were limited by others is clear in her comments.

These interviewees are not alone in these views. Cliff (mid-twenties, first generation), for example, stated that "we as Asians could not go into the YMCA. We were condemned to play outdoors, being Asian, being yellow" (September 2006). Furthermore, during the Washington tournament, a player who was acting as a court monitor was explaining the rationale for the eligibility rules to a spectator by retelling this well-worn story of exclusion from sports. He ended with, "So they just want to keep it Chinese, *which I can understand*" (emphasis added) and to which the spectator responded, "Yeah, totally." Both individuals agreed that the eligibility rules are justified in light of the racism that was experienced by Chinese people when the tournament began. Although a number of interviewees made reference to past victimization and racism as a rationale for the eligibility rules and for the existence of the NACIVT, one individual who had been involved in the tournament since the 1950s stated that he was not sure how true these stories of discrimination were. In his recollection, by the time he began playing, his team did not experience barriers to accessing space. In sharing his perspective, I am not suggesting that the story of victimization is not true. Rather, it reinforces how this history of discrimination is presumed to be a solid reference point and stable position from which to speak.

Participants also mobilized this sense of shared victimhood through presenting the NACIVT as a safe haven from being stereotyped and encountering what Leo called "racial challenges, stereotypical challenges." He believed that the tournament provided space for the mediocre Asian volleyball player who, in other leagues, would be judged and stereotyped as "Asian people suck at volleyball," whereas in the NACIVT, "we're all Asian, we all sucked at one point," and thus there would be greater understanding and empathy rather than stereotyping. John further pointed out how stereotypes operate in volleyball. He explained that Asian volleyball players are presumed to excel only at defence in the backcourt and setting, and to have limited offensive capabilities because of shorter stature. The NACIVT, then, provides a space where players are not limited by these stereotypes and expectations and can perform as powerful hitters and blockers. This finding mirrors Carrington's (1998) discussion of how a cricket club became a Black space where "Black people could be themselves (for example, in being able to tell certain jokes and speak in Caribbean patois), free from the structures imposed by the White gaze" (284; see also Chin 2016).

In the literature, there are other examples of seeking co-ethnic sports spaces as a "safe haven" from racism and discrimination.

Howell (1995) writes, for example, that the sporting activities of Blacks in Maritime Canada provided a sense of camaraderie in light of the discrimination they faced (see also Carrington 1998; Humber 1995; Thangaraj 2013, 2015a, 2015b). An overview of the establishment of an Ecuadorian soccer league also discusses the difficulties that immigrants encountered upon arrival in Ontario, including the shared sense of "discontent, uncertainty and fear" (Romero 1985, 29), and how participating in the Ecuadorian soccer league helped alleviate these anxieties. Similarly, Yep (2009) found that despite their paltry resources, Chinese American basketball players in San Francisco's Chinatown were empowered because their style of play, even when represented in the media in ways that reproduced stereotypes (i.e., players are speedy, short, and excel in defence), helped to shift dominant views about Chinese people. Similarly, Thangaraj (2013, 2015a, 2015b) found that the South Asian American basketball players in his study are marginalized within mainstream basketball, not simply in relation to Blackness and Whiteness as the "natural" or "normal" bodies that may take up sports, but also because of a post-9/11 context where Brown men are constructed as terrorists and therefore expelled from the nation entirely. Their participation in a co-ethnic sporting space, then, is in part "to escape the racist sentiments they experience in other multiracial arenas" (Thangaraj, 2015a, 16).

The marginalization of Asian players within and exclusion from mainstream White volleyball structures needs to be contextualized within a history of such exclusion. Scholars have noted the examples of the exclusion of Asian people from sports and recreation in the United States (e.g., Yep 2009; Chin 2012; Willms 2010). With the strong connection between sports and citizenship (i.e., that participation in sports is an expression of citizenship), it is significant that Asian people in particular were excluded from sports (Nakamura 2012). Lowe (1996) argues that the American institution of citizenship necessitated the legal exclusion and disenfranchisement of Asian immigrants, making their citizenship within national culture an impossibility. This is especially true in the case of Chinese in Canada and the United States, since they were excluded from entering these nations, or forced to pay an entry tax because of race. They have, therefore, been constructed outside of the nation, historically barred from its soil and its citizenry (see also Leung & Guan 2004; Li 2003b). The internment of Japanese people in Canada and the United States, despite the fact that two-thirds of interned Japanese Americans were naturalized citizens and documented evidence in Canada that Japanese people were not a security threat, also illustrates how Asians have been treated as less than citizens.

In light of the historical links between physical education and nation-building (Okay 2003; McNeill, Sproule, & Horton 2003), the fact that Chinese men were perceived not to belong in recreational spaces at the time of the early beginnings of the NACIVT as well as the continued perception that Asians do not belong in physical education spaces (Millington et al. 2008) are manifestations of the exclusion of Asian bodies from the nation, in both the United States and Canada (Park 2007). Thus, as a way to justify the rule, the interviewees took a position of victimhood not just in remembrance of a recent past but also as a response to the legacy of exclusion from the nation and categorization as Other. Nevertheless, this stance is premised on the assumption that exclusion is justified if one is a marginalized group, and risks falling into the trap of competing marginalities as each group vies to be the most marginalized and limits the potential for making allies (Razack & Fellows 1998).

The meaning of this strategy of solidarity also needs to be contextualized within the time period when the majority of the interviews were taking place. In Canada, for example, Chinese people were increasingly being criticized for supposedly "unCanadian" practices and for causing various social problems, from "monopolizing spaces in medical schools to driving up real estate prices in Vancouver to establishing ethnic enclaves in the Greater Toronto Area" (Fleras 2011, 22). Shortly before the interviews began, the SARS outbreak occurred (in 2003), resulting in the demonizing of Chinese people as the cause of the disease and in anxiety towards Asian people in general caused by fear of catching the disease. This particular issue was raised in an entry on 11 June 2003 in the guestbook of the now-defunct tournament website, where one individual asked, "Would we, as North Americans of Chinese (Asian) heritage, be 'scrutinized' as Japanese-Americans were [in] WWII?" This statement reflects a context in which individuals may have felt united or at the very least equally targeted as a result of SARS, illustrating how past (and the potential of ongoing) victimization serves to stabilize the community and erase difference since "we all know there are enough battles to fight on the outside" (*NACIVT.com guestbook*, n.d.).

This final statement is particularly demonstrative of the risks of deploying this particular strategy for solidarity. When the community is constructed as homogeneous, the diversity within the NACIVT and, most importantly, the hierarchies within it are neglected. Consequently, the needs of those marginalized within the community are ignored or denied. Critics of the Asian American movement have pointed out that treating Asian Americans as a homogeneous group hid the reality that American-born, middle-class, and primarily Chinese and/or Japanese people were speaking for the community; similarly, within the NACIVT, positioning the tournament, the eligibility rules, and the participants in this way serves to elide the contemporary culture of middle classness that permeates the tournament, one that is far from its working-class roots, and, most importantly, conceals the racial logic upon which membership, identity, and belonging are defined and naturalized. This racial logic was described as follows by Rob: "The thinking was, you know, Japanese and Koreans, we can be as good as them (laughs), but boy don't bring in those *gweilos* [White people], we could really lose (laughs)." Rob laughed heartily as he described the rationale for maintaining the status quo, and when he joked that *gweilos* were particularly unwelcome. But "Whiteness" and its presumed biology, physiology, and athleticism, though socially constructed, are serious matters within the NACIVT.

When the conversation turned to the topic of the eligibility rules and the need for these boundaries, interviewees regularly and consistently referred to White people and their potential incursion into the NACIVT. Specifically, participants would speak of White volleyball players – their presumed greater height and related superior abilities – and the resultant limiting of the opportunities for Asian volleyball players (racialized as short) to play at an elite level if the tournament were opened to all. In other words, they drew on discourses of biological racism and essentialism, believing that certain groups are more or less endowed with athletic abilities, and that their inherent identities are reflected in their race and reinforced by the demonstration of their physicality. Rachel (19 years old, second generation), for example, stated that "your race sort of dictates in your genes what type of abilities you have," and so she perceived that "if people did start joining, that were from other races, [the tournament] would change."

A number of interviewees, such as Carol and Peter, expressed the importance of maintaining the eligibility rules so that weaker, less-skilled volleyball players would still be able to participate. Kyle (28 years old, second generation) agreed, stating that the NACIVT was for the

> guys that didn't play varsity or guys that can't make it pro which is the majority of everybody ... this is it. [...] For the guys that aren't so good, it's just the fact that they get to do something active, play something that they probably love, just unfortunately they're not that good at it, but they get to still play.

Mark also felt that some "Asian" players "might not have the opportunity to play volleyball at a – that type of representative level if other people were coming in, if outsiders were coming in."

Owen was more explicit, stating that removing the rule would limit opportunities for "Chinese" players because they are generally shorter. He was not alone in this view. Eli speculated that "the full Chinese teams will, if they're sticking with the full Chinese, then they will be left out of [the tournament], even just with the size. Because [the nine-man players] play on a lower net, it gives the taller people a much bigger advantage." Further, Mark suggested that "Asian" players would be relegated to the back row "because at the end of the day, you're looking at size and ... and Asians just don't grow that big." Phoebe highlighted one particular player in order to demonstrate this point. She described this athlete as unbelievable and yet she is only able to play libero at the NCAA level. You know she can hit a ball as hard as any of them, but because she's short she can't play front row against all the other tall players, right? So if we open this up to everybody, not only do we lose, you know, tradition ... but we also end up losing a lot of front-row positions to taller people.

The libero position is that of a defensive specialist who is not able to block or attack the ball when it is above the net. Phoebe gave this example to demonstrate that although this player is exceptional and powerful within the NACIVT, outside the NACIVT and within the NCAA level of play she is limited to defence because she is not effective against "all the other tall players." Thus, to open up the tournament would result in limiting the playing positions and opportunities of even highly skilled players. Other interviewees went even further and believed that "Asian" players would not be able to continue playing at all in the tournament if the eligibility rules were not in place. This explanation is grounded in biological racism, whereby height serves as a "structuring principle" (Mukharji 2008, 274) to organize bodies and the format of the NACIVT.

The issue of height has also been raised in other leagues and contexts. For example, King-O'Riain observed that the Bay Area Nikkei League had a rule that players who have no Japanese ancestry may participate in the basketball league provided the player or the player's parent(s) were active members of a sponsoring Japanese organization, and the player was not recruited as a ringer and was not over six feet tall. Japanese players were defined as having any Japanese ancestry, and could play irrespective of height, suggesting that the definition of Japaneseness was far more fluid and flexible than in the NACIVT rulebook. In reality, though, as with the mixed-race players in the NACIVT, mixed-race Japanese Americans were questioned about their legitimacy (King-O'Riain 2002; see also Chin 2012).

Height (dis)advantage and tradition were linked, in that the latter was used to prevent the former. This discursive connection is demonstrated in Phoebe's comment quoted above, as well as

Kyle's explanation for the need for eligibility rules. He states that a team that has a majority of tall players would have an edge over "a team that has 100 per cent Chinese shorter players [...] So I think that's where the rule is important, because if you want to keep tradition and you want to keep it fair, you gotta have that stipulation, and if it was open to everybody, it wouldn't really be a sport, I guess, for Asians, for Chinese." Kyle therefore contradicts himself by suggesting that the rule is to maintain tradition when, by his own admission, it is to prevent a height advantage and to ensure that "Chinese" and "Asian" players have a fair chance to win. Thus, tradition is being used as a cover for a rationale grounded in biological racism.

While height has been named as a justification for boundaries and to maintain "a height-controlled environment" (Willms 2010, 227), one should also be sensitive to how height is structured through racism and gender. In an ethnography of a high school, Lei found that the lack of height was a critical factor in determining the low status of Southeast Asian American males within the school hierarchy. Because the norm was taken to be the "white, European American, abled, and athletic male body, which demands a higher height (the average being around five feet eleven inches) and stockier build, the average physique of the Southeast Asian American male student was constituted as small and weak" (Lei 2003, 172–3). Consequently, the masculinity of students of Southeast Asian background was being marginalized. A lack of height was also interpreted in infantilizing ways, where shorter men were seen as children. It was also used as an explanation for Southeast Asian males' lack of interest in sports or for an expectation that they should be playing sports that did not require height. While Lei focused on the relationship between height and "Asian masculinity," the racialization of height likely has broader effects. Willms (2010) argues that height serves as a euphemism for race – that one can speak of the short stature of "Asian" people, in lieu of race, and yet the effect is a racialization of "Asian" people (see also Chin 2012). Thus, a focus on height likely serves to perpetuate the assumption that "Asian" women are frail and docile and would shy away from sports.

Across the interviews, "White" volleyball players were consistently perceived as potentially more skilled than "Asian" players. Lisa (29 years old, second generation) admitted that removing the rule would be a good way to promote the sport of nine-man and of volleyball more generally, but said, "You know if you include Caucasians or whatever, [you would] get completely overshadowed by Caucasians." Likewise, when asked what changes to the eligibility rules he could foresee, Peter responded that "it probably won't change the part where you're not allowed having Caucasians [...] because then a lot of these Asians wouldn't be playing. A lot of them would not be good enough to play." Nancy pointed out that in teams outside the NACIVT, even if a team was composed of all "Asian" players, "you'll get the ringer as the token White person on our team," suggesting that "White" players are presumed to be more skilled athletes. This was reinforced by a coach who explained that his team competed in a league outside the NACIVT during the regular season. He stated that the NACIVT team he coaches stays together (i.e., are all "Asian" players) and that his team was faring very well. He then made a point of telling me that the team he was coaching was "playing against all Caucasian girls," reinforcing the assumption that "Caucasian" women are better than "Asian" volleyball players; or that while remaining an all-"Asian" team could potentially make them less competitive compared to all-"Caucasian" teams, they are still winning. In either case, the standard against which the team's success is being measured is that of all-"Caucasian" teams.

While "White" players are perceived as the primary threat against which the NACIVT needs to protect itself, there are players who have been read as "White" who have participated in past tournaments, such as Michael's recollection of a team that had a "Caucasian" player. Later, I learned that this player was included in the roster because the team in question did not have enough ("Asian") players to field a team. Thus, there have been occasions where "White" players have participated and have been welcomed, although these examples are rare and the individuals have usually been good but not dominant players. Despite these few counterexamples, the data seem to suggest that the greatest threat was perceived to be having "White" people participate in the NACIVT and the potential impact this would have on the tournament. This is illustrated by a conversation overheard during the Washington tournament between a player and a spectator who was unfamiliar with the tournament. The spectator asked about the rules and was surprised to learn that there were guidelines restricting participation around "race." He asked, "Is that so the Whites don't come in and ruin it? (laughs)." Most interviewees felt that the inclusion of White players would result in "Asian" people playing an increasingly minor role on teams and ultimately being pushed out of the tournament. This view is likely related to the US and Canadian contexts in which the players participated, and the "Whiteness" of volleyball in these contexts.

Just as Chin (2012) and Willms (2010) found that how basketball was racialized as "Black" shaped the Japanese Americans' experience of the sport, the frequent reference to "White" volleyball players and their participation as threatening to the NACIVT is surely related to how volleyball is perceived as "White." For example, in a discussion of what rules he would like to see changed, Peter stated that he would like the nets to be raised in nine-man. At present, the net "is lower on the men's side, but on the women's, it's the same as Caucasian." That he said "Caucasian," rather than "International" or "FIVB" is evidence that "Whiteness" is the norm. Furthermore, interviewees frequently pointed out how their volleyball experiences were dominated by "White" players. Karen, for instance, described how the club volleyball system in her region reflects "a predominantly White sport." Interviewees such as Nancy or Phoebe who were involved in intercollegiate-level volleyball also recalled how the school team "was all White" (Nancy) or that the local club volleyball league had "a lot more White people" (Phoebe).

The perceived "Whiteness" of volleyball is not simply a result of more "White" people being drawn to the sport. Volleyball is rooted in a history of imperialism through its relationship to the Young Men's Christian Association (YMCA). The game was invented in 1895 by William G. Morgan, director of physical education at the YMCA in Holyoke, Massachusetts. It was created out of a need for an activity for older men, one that was less violent and less strenuous than basketball. The new game quickly spread across the world through the various YMCA schools and societies in Canada, the Philippines, China, Japan, Burma (Myanmar), India, and several Latin American countries (McGehee 1997; "Chronological highlights" n.d.; "Volleyball history" n.d.).

What is not mentioned in the FIVB chronology of volleyball is the history of the YMCA's project of mission work, imperialism, and the perceived role of volleyball in building the character of foreign and immigrant men and spreading muscular Christianity, or the "Christian commitment to health and manliness" (Putney 2001, 11). When the United States colonized the Philippines, the YMCA worked closely with the colonial government to ensure that the sports curriculum would civilize "the natives," uplift those who were deemed inferior, and impart American values. Volleyball in particular was seen as an ideal vehicle for teaching values like democracy, teamwork, sacrifice for the good of the whole, obedience to a coach, and a strong work ethic (Gems 1999). In the case of China, the YMCA began its civilizing mission in Tianjin in 1895 (Morris 2000). While it intended to spread Christianity, it also hoped to "recreate the superior 'Anglo-Saxon' American society of free trade, democracy, liberty, republicanism, and science" (Morris 2000, 889); to spread a civilizing culture in Asia; and to bring "Chinese men and their nation into the Western and modern fold" (892). Thus, volleyball and the YMCA are rooted in an imperial "program of normalization" (892).

Though the imperializing and colonizing imperative of volleyball may be less explicit now, for many of the interviewees, mainstream volleyball remained primarily a "White" space. They articulated feelings and experiences of being the lone "Asian" player on their high-school or intercollegiate team. Even smaller recreational mainstream volleyball leagues were perceived to be "usually all White people" (Christie). Nancy, for example, recalled how her school team "was all White." She said, "I was the only Asian on the team, and the second year, there were two Asians, but I was the only Asian that actually got to play." John also noted that on his team there was perhaps one other player of Asian descent, and "all the rest were Caucasian. Like there's nobody else." He recalled feeling "singled out, 'Oh, yeah, the Chinese guy [John]' or whatever." His last comment illustrates how his lone status reinforced how he was racialized as Chinese, despite being of a different ethnicity (i.e., "All Asians are the same"; "they are all Chinese," and so on). This racial breakdown was no different during his participation in club-level volleyball. He explained that it was "probably 90 per cent Caucasian in the [Regional] Volleyball Association and then there's a minuscule amount of African Americans, and 5 per cent or less of Asian players. So it's actually quite hard to find anybody [Asian]."

This lack of Asian volleyball players was noted by other interviewees. Kyle "was maybe one of two or three Asians in the whole city [who played competitive volleyball], and all I played with was non-Asians, majority Caucasian." Lisa also stated that she was one of a few Asian players who participated in the volleyball club system, but she was quick to state that "I never felt like I was different or I never felt that in a sea of White girls I was any different." However, she later described how

It's very obvious when you go into a tournament in [a smaller, racially homogeneous city] and you know … of the 200 young girls that are there, you are the only Asian and it's *very* obvious. But you know I got used to it with time.

Lisa, at first, claims that she did not feel different when she played volleyball. It is interesting, though, that she described her surroundings as a "sea of White girls," suggesting she was conscious that most other players were "White." Furthermore, Lisa notes that she became accustomed to this situation, indicating that her lone "Asian" status did not change over time. This awareness of being the only "Asian" among predominantly "White" players in turn led to internalizing racial stereotypes (see also Y. Lee, 2015). For example, having successfully competed among "Caucasian" players for most of his volleyball career, Kyle joked that when he first learned about the NACIVT, he assumed that he was "probably better than any other Asians out there." John also had similar expectations when he first learned of the NACIVT.

The dominance of "White" volleyball players, the lack of "Asian" players within mainstream volleyball systems, and the stereotyping of "Asian" players may limit "Asian" people's ability to access mainstream volleyball teams. This struggle is reflected in Christie's attempt to join a Regional Volleyball Association [RVA] team when she was 18:

> I think that the RVA is racist too. If you're not five foot ten, [with] blonde hair and blue eyes, you will not make an RVA team. Okay, I'm generalizing and making assumptions, but honestly, [...] when I tried out, they know that I had skill, but I wasn't tall enough. And that was when I was 18, just trying to get into RVA.

Christie proceeded to explain that a few years later she was approached by RVA players who admired her skill and talent and was asked what RVA team she played for, assuming that she must have developed her abilities in the mainstream volleyball system. She recounted with pride how surprised these players were to learn that she had never played on an RVA team and that it was her NACIVT coach who saw her potential and took the time to mould her into a highly skilled volleyball player. Similarly, Luke (38 years old, second generation) recalled how his high-school team was being scouted by RVA teams and that

> I never, I never got an offer. No one really wanted to take me under their wing and this other guy got taken. And you know I hate to think of it this way, um [...] I thought maybe it was because I was Asian (laugh). And he's a Caucasian dude.

Despite being co-captain and highly skilled, Luke was not invited to join an RVA club team. While he can only speculate that "race" was a reason for his lack of opportunities, there is no doubt that the mainstream volleyball system remained closed to him, whereas he was welcomed easily into the NACIVT. With the pervasive view that White people are taller, stronger, and better volleyball players, and that mainstream volleyball is a White space where few Asians can enter, it is not surprising that discussion of the eligibility rules invariably turns to "White" athleticism being the greatest threat.

The perceived greater advantage and therefore threat of White athleticism is best illustrated by the discussion of half-White mixed-race individuals' participation in the NACIVT. The apparent danger that these individuals pose is inextricably linked to ideas of bloodline, genetics, and purity. Unlike a "full Asian" player, those whose bodies are not read as "100 per cent" or "pure" are more likely to be deemed a threat to the opposing team precisely because of the "impure" element that could make them a better jumper, a stronger hitter, or a faster digger. For example, one player felt that height was a key advantage gained from being of mixed (genetic) heritage. He named two mixed-race "Asian" players in the NACIVT and said, "They're six foot six, six foot eight. Where'd they get that from? Maybe Asian ancestry (said dubiously)?" Mark made similar remarks, suggesting that "half-Asian" players would be taller and referred to a team from the United States that had a number of "half-Chinese on the team and they're giants." Kyle was far more explicit about the potential unfairness of being mixed race, particularly "half-White":

> When it becomes, "[I am] half-Chinese and half something else," there could be an advantage in that. But that could possibly take away from the people that are 100 per cent Chinese right? A lot of the times, the odds are when you're 100 per cent Chinese, the odds aren't really in your favour of being tall, for example. But say you're a mix of, say, Chinese and something else, say, like Caucasian, for example, you have a better chance of being tall. So if you have a team that has a majority of tall players versus a team that has 100 per cent Chinese shorter players, there, the advantage [of being 100 per cent Chinese] that's lost.

Clearly, it is the "non-Asian/Chinese half" that poses a possible threat to a "100 per cent Chinese" team. Purity, then, is symbolized by conformity to stereotypical ideas about what an "Asian" body looks like and what an "Asian" body is capable of doing, both of which are perceived to be determined entirely by genetic background.

In addition to height, Diane explained that "when you get mixed players, like if they're half-White, half-Chinese, their technique is better, they're stronger. Like if you have a White background, you're technically stronger." John also felt that mixed-race "Asian" players had a higher calibre of play, calling on professional athletes like "Heinz Ward who's half-Korean and Tiger Woods who's half-Filipino [sic]." While he was not trying to imply that "full Asian people are not becoming great athletes, but if you look at the people in the NFL, MLB, Tiger Woods in golf, that is a big population of Asian players that are helping to grow the game." In his study, Mukharji (2008) argues that imagined racial difference between "slightly built Bengalis and muscular big boned Africans [...] has animated the drive to recruit African players" (275) into a Bengali football club. There is no such drive to recruit "half-White" players into the NACIVT because of the eligibility rules. In fact, Mark recalled a time when a proposal was made to ban the participation of "half-Asian" players, perhaps because they were deemed so threatening. The proposal was that "if you were half but you weren't half-Chinese, you wouldn't be able to play [...] But if you were full, you could be full anything, full Korean, full Japanese, or whatever, you were able to play" (Mark). This call for change was rejected "pretty easily just because everyone had players that were half something" (Mark).

It is conceivable that "full" but multi-ethnic Asian players would likely have been permitted to play had this rule come to pass. Although the invisibility of "Chineseness" as ethnicity among those "Asian" players who are able to "pass" as "Chinese" through using ethnic strategies like last name can be a source of discomfort, the visibility of race serves to make such players less threatening when their bodies are read through this lens. There may be an element of being able to blend in that works in favour of those who are of multi-ethnic parentage but are "fully Asian," a fact that may explain why, for instance, interviewees seemed to focus on the eligibility rules that limited the playing time or impact of "half-Asian" players. This position was best illustrated by a comment made by an individual who had been associated with the tournament for several years. When asked to identify the challenges he had faced over the years as a player and a coach, without hesitation he responded that the primary obstacle was the increasing number of mixed-race "Asian" players. He proceeded to claim that the tournament was "strictly Chinese before. If we see too many violations, maybe then we might have to go back to just Chinese." In other words, the "part-Asian, part-Other" players and their growing presence in the tournament had led to violations of the eligibility rule, and if this continued, he believed that the tournament should return to an all-"Chinese" format. Rather than questioning the rules, problematizing coaches who tried to undermine the rules by including too many "non-100 per cent Chinese," or faulting referees who did not enforce the rules, this individual placed the blame squarely on the "part-Asian" players.

The biological racism that sees physical and athletic difference as innate is the foundation upon which the belief that the participation of mixed-race, half-White/half-Asian players should be constrained if not limited is based. Thus, while socially constructed biological racial difference serves to raise up "half-White players" as more talented and athletic, it also simultaneously diminishes the place of "half-White" players in the NACIVT. This contradictory status of "half-White" players in the NACIVT illustrates the limits of what King-O'Riain (2006) calls the "transracial ethnic strategy" (121). She proposes this option as a way for the Asian American community, threatened by the increase in mixed-race Asian people and the potential impact this would have on solidarity and the size of their community, to include multiracial Asian people. Rather than the option of assimilating or forming a panethnicity, she suggests that this third option entails "accept[ing] mixed-race members over and above other Asian ethnics" (123). This approach, she suggested, "recognizes ethnic differences while transcending racial lines" (131). However, in a later publication she concludes that mixed-race people are not "leading us into a world of fewer racial meanings, but instead into a world of increasing 'race work' that aims to prop up racial concepts using culture, gender, and community networks as scaffolding" (20; see also Christian 2011; Yu 2002). Certainly, this would seem to be the case with how "half-White, half-Asian" players are viewed in the NACIVT and constructed into a combination of two discrete and separate races. Their bodies and their abilities are understood in relation to and in support of these racial categories. Interestingly, where, outside of sports, mixed-race people are now admired and/or exoticized for their hybrid physical appearance and "cool" status, or celebrated as the future of a post-racial society (Dagbovie 2007), within the NACIVT sporting contexts where racial identities are negotiated and contested (Y. Lee, 2005), mixed-race people are essentialized in relation to narrow, monoracial categories, which are in turn triangulated within a broader racial context (Kim 1999).

Kim (1999) refers to this relative positioning and social construction of racial groups as "a field of racial positions" (106) whereby each racial position is determined in relation to others, such as that of Asian Americans in relation to Black and White people. She illustrates how "Asian Americans specifically have been 'racially triangulated' vis-à-vis whites and blacks in this field of racial positions" (106) in that Asian American people have been simultaneously valorized in relation to Black people via the model minority myth, while still being rejected from the body politic because they are constructed as foreign and unassimilable. Racial triangulation can also be applied to the sporting context. For example, Willms (2010) examines Japanese American basketball leagues in California and suggests that, in that particular context, both cultural and biological triangulation occurs. First, cultural triangulation occurs via the assumption that Asian Americans are culturally superior to African American people and thus would not over-invest in sports (Willms 2010). However, where sports participation for White youth is seen as an important extracurricular activity to demonstrate well-roundedness, Asian Americans are presumed to not value sports and thus "are symbolically excluded from this version of [sports]" participation as a valuable accomplishment (Willms 2010). Second, biological triangulation in sports, according to Willms, entails constructing Asian Americans as less athletically gifted compared to the "natural" Black athlete, and as short of stature compared to White people.

In the NACIVT, racial triangulation via biological and cultural triangulation was less apparent. Certainly, greater height was predominantly linked to Whiteness and, in turn, Asian athleticism was constructed in relation to Whiteness, its greater height, and subsequent volleyball advantage. As Sarah put it, "nobody ever looks at me and thinks, 'She's an athlete that plays volleyball.'" Through high-level coaching and intense practices, the NACIVT provides opportunities for "athletes who don't fit the cookie-cutter mould of six feet tall, five foot eleven volleyball players" (Christie) who dominate mainstream White volleyball leagues and circuits. For example, Christie remarked that an increasing number of NACIVT players who are below or just six feet are playing key roles on men's intercollegiate volleyball teams, an observation echoed by Patrick. Christie believes that through the NACIVT, "they've had the opportunity to learn technique and training so they can get their vertical that tall or get their blocks down so they can compete against guys who are six foot five. So that's a big difference." In the mainstream high-school or RVA teams, "Asian" players may not get the chance even to make the team, let alone learn and develop their skills. In fact, for many of the interviewees, the draw of being part of a team that competed in the NACIVT was the chance to experience formal practices led by a coach with drills and scrimmages, something that many of the interviewees did not have access to through secondary or post-secondary schooling, let alone through club volleyball programs. Christie believes that it is precisely because of the training received in the NACIVT that her teammates have been able to receive accolades within the mainstream volleyball system, such as Rookie of the Year, or to succeed in competitive volleyball such as international beach volleyball tours and intercollegiate sport.

The triangulation of Asianness/Whiteness/Blackness within the NACIVT leaned heavily towards Whiteness in that the interviewees did not seem to see themselves or their volleyball experiences in relation to Blackness. This finding is particularly interesting, since Blackness is overdetermined by assumptions of naturally gifted athleticism or, in other words, by the very same biological essentialism through which the interviewees understood their own athletic abilities or lack thereof. This is not to say that Blackness does not figure into the physical activity and sports experiences of Asian people. Lei (2003) found, for instance, that racial tension with Black students was the reason a group of Southeast Asian American male high school students were not more involved in sports. In the case of the NACIVT, the omission of Blackness may be related to the Whiteness of volleyball and to the fact that there is "a minuscule [... number] of African Americans" (John) in the mainstream volleyball systems in which the interviewees participate. Another person noted how, in other leagues in which her team plays, the players are "usually all White people," except for "one all Black team" and her entirely Chinese team. The implication of this relationship between the athleticism of Asian and White people helps to shift the discussion of race away from "its usual Black and White chromatism" (Mukharji 2008, 284). Instead, it becomes clear how tropes of race "[generate] a matrix of meanings and commonsense in which feeble Bengalis and sturdy Africans complement and mutually define each other, along with artful Brazilians, deft Iranians, persevering Britons" (284), short Asians, and tall Whites.

Cultural triangulation within sports as outlined by Willms (2010) highlights how Asianness, Whiteness, and Blackness are constructed in relation to each other via assumed cultural values. Among the NACIVT participants, rather than praising Asian values, the participants demonstrated an awareness of the prevalent stereotype of Asian people as studious bookworms rather than vigorous athletes, or of Asian men as effeminate and Asian women as frail and unfit (King 2015). Sarah, for example, described her participation in the NACIVT as breaking "from the normal stereotype of Asians not playing sports you know or musical [...] or like good at math." Nevertheless, rejecting cultural assumptions and stereotypes did not go any further, and while the NACIVT interviewees did not explicitly name Blackness, the positioning of Asianness in relation to Whiteness makes clear how participation in sports is understood as a path to demonstrating good citizenship and gaining social status. The significance of being skilled at sports as a marker of social status (Bourdieu 1978; White & McTeer 1990), one that is gained by performing "Whiteness," is reflected in Michael's story of his son and his experiences in sports:

> My son is very smart and very capable. You know when he was in high school, he was a good student. He gets As. But he doesn't participate in sport. He says "The only way I could outdo the Caucasians is through sport because that's the only thing they look at. They know the Chinese is smart." So he played baseball and football and he became a good player. So now he gains the confidence. "I can beat you in anything." You know so [the NACIVT] is one way for us to take pride in ourselves, and say "Hey, we're good at something," have that knowledge.

According to Michael, his son recognized the limits of staying within the confines of the model minority, and saw playing sports as a way to gain recognition and confidence and, I would suggest, social status.

Later, Michael explained that his family was the first Chinese family to move into the neighbourhood where his children grew up. When his son began attending school, Michael asked him if there were other Chinese children in his class. His son responded, "What do they look like?" Michael laughingly said that, at the time, his son did not know he was Chinese. Clearly, he later came to understand himself and who Chinese people were in relation to "Caucasian" students, based on stereotypes that were imposed and voluntarily taken up. Thus, the NACIVT provides an opportunity for his son and for other "Asian" players to debunk these stereotypes and to illustrate that they are more than academics and model minorities – that they can also be skilled and confident athletes. In other words, Asianness was positioned in relation to the trope of being well-rounded, a virtue that White youth are able to enjoy when they are involved in various activities and from which Asian youth are usually excluded because of assumptions about culture.

Gender

What is missing from the discussion of cultural and racial triangulation in sport is how this relational positioning is gendered and classed. Kim's (1999) concept of racial triangulation is insightful in that citizenship and the status of Asianness are understood vis-à-vis emulation of (but never full acceptance in) Whiteness but also differentiation from Blackness. Citizenship, though, is also a gendered, heteronormative, and classed construct, such that those who are women, queer, or working class are not accorded automatic inclusion in the body politic. In some ways, sports participation offers a way to reaffirm a sense of identity and belonging, particularly for gendered and racialized identities that are constructed as Other. For example, Carrington (1998), in his study of a cricket club, found that participation was a source of Black masculine pride and a way to restore racial identity, critical for a community that continues to be marginalized and disenfranchised.

Similarly, Asian men in the NACIVT may also use their involvement as a way to reclaim their racial, masculine identities. Asian boys are conscious of being stereotyped as non-athletic (Nakamura 2004), just as men in this study were. As Fung (1996) demonstrates, Asian men are emasculated through the interlocking of racism and hegemonic masculinity (see also Kumashiro 1999; Lei 2003). Up until the shift in demographic profile of the tournament (chapter 1), Chinese American and Canadian men's lives would also be framed by their working-class contexts and, for some, their feminized labour. Carl (early forties, second generation), a former player who remained involved as a coach and organizer, described watching his father and his teammates play. He said how "earning a living back then was fight, fight, fight," and that he could see this mentality being played out on the court. Bourdieu writes about the intersection of class and sports culture, suggesting that for working-class people, there is a relationship of class to the body and the choice of sport in that the choice of activity requires tremendous effort, or even experiences of pain and suffering. Even the risk to the body may be indicative of what Bourdieu (1978) identifies as another manifestation of the relationship of class to the body seen among the working classes. Nonetheless, as Chen (1999, 589) points out, Chinese American (and likely Chinese Canadian) men "live at the center and periphery of" intersecting systems of oppression. Thus, Chinese American and Canadian men for whom hegemonic masculinity is not easily accessible enter into a hegemonic bargain, trading privileges that arise from the intersection of race, gender, sexuality, class, and generation in order to achieve masculinity (Chen 1999). For Chinese American and Canadian men in the NACIVT who were emasculated by race and their feminized labour, playing nine-man volleyball aggressively outside on the streets likely offered an opportunity to trade in working-class values to recuperate their masculinity.

In the case of the NACIVT, participation is a way to recover traditional masculinity for men, as it was for the Hong Wah Kues, the Chinese American barnstorming basketball team in Yep's (2009) study, who "challenged racist stereotypes by presenting an empowered version of Chinese American masculinity" (61) via basketball (see also Thangaraj 2013, 2015a, 2015b). Yep's text illustrates how this empowerment occurs within and in relation to the harsh reality of intersecting oppressions (i.e., poverty, patriarchy, and racism) via basketball. The text is valuable because it focuses on a time period (the 1930s and 1940s) and a community whose sports experiences have been neglected until quite recently.

In the case of South Asian American men, however, Thangaraj (2013, 2015a, 2015b) found that the masculinity they constructed through basketball relied on and reproduced conservative ideas about gender, class, and sexuality, the very constructs that marginalized them in the first place. In light of the invention of volleyball as a less strenuous and less violent game and its representation as less manly (in the hegemonic sense) because of the lack of physical contact and violence (Ken, John), in the NACIVT a different form of masculinity is being formulated (A. Wang 2000). Nonetheless, just as Thangaraj (2015a) found that the South Asian American masculinity cultivated within exclusively Brown basketball spaces was not transportable outside of such spaces, the sense of belonging and citizenship cultivated via the NACIVT, whether in hegemonic or alternative ways, may not extend beyond the boundaries of the NACIVT. Clearly, racial and cultural triangulation in sports intersects with other categories of oppression.

The threat of Whiteness operates differently in the women's games during the NACIVT in large part because the women play the sixes game. As there are only two spots that are available for "non-100 per cent Chinese" participants, players must compete for fewer spots. However, the threat from "Other" players is arguably less in the women's game because of the practice of rotation. Unlike nine-man, all six players on the court must rotate to a different position on the court each time the team earns a serve. Any tall player, therefore, would not always play at the net, blocking every shot or attacking every set. Instead, she would rotate to the backcourt position where blocks or attacks are not permitted. Thus, how race operates within the women's games must be understood within the context of the sixes game and of their exclusion from nines, which is justified and explained by biological essentialism and the social construction of women's "nature" and biology.

Biological essentialism provides the justification for excluding women from nines in a way that strongly parallels the anxiety about "White" athleticism. For example, a former player explained that "women cannot get the height" to play nines. By this, he was referring to being able to jump high enough to do some of the moves that are characteristic of the nines game, such as throwing the ball. James, too, felt that women simply were not tall enough to play the game at a high level. While they might be exceptional athletes and highly skilled in women's sixes, he said that "getting the size to play the nines style would be difficult." He went on to explain that the nines game is

> a very fast-paced game based on power and quickness and when you compare women's sixes and men's sixes, men's game is more explosive, and you get a quick bump-set-kill, whereas women's game is traditionally more a rally.

While he acknowledged that women players had excellent technical skills that would be applicable in the nines game, he did not think there were any women active in the NACIVT at the time who could produce "the kind of explosive power and speed that you would need in the nines men's game." Ultimately, James seemed conflicted as to whether women could play nines. He recognized that there are a number of outstanding women volleyball players in the NACIVT and yet implied that biological reasons such as limited jumping ability and lack of height, power, and speed would prevent women from excelling or even playing the nines game. James was not alone in this inconsistency. Christie also felt that biology could limit women's ability to play nine-man because it is a very fast-paced game. She did not think women are fast, athletic, or powerful enough to play nines. However, she was quick to call this her own ignorance and stated that she had watched mediocre men's teams and thought to herself that she could play better than some of the players.

In addition, Lisa expressed ambivalence about the question of whether women could play nines. She said her immediate response would be, "Hell, yeah, you can if you *want* to, I mean who's to say that you can't?" Lisa then considered the possibility for a moment and elaborated on how women fared against men:

> women can probably play defence just as well you know as a male could and certainly setting, I'm an example of that where I'm probably the same height as some of the [male] setters (laughs) that are already setting on the circuit.

Despite her initial reaction that women could most definitely play nines, she too drew on biological essentialism, citing physical constraints such as lack of height, speed, and strength as potentially limiting women's nines abilities. Thus, the question of whether women could play nines did initially elicit explanations that were grounded in biological reasoning – such as that women are shorter, slower, and weaker than men – but also comments recognizing women's talent and abilities. This recognition, though, is tenuous and is only a recent phenomenon. For the most part, women athletes in the NACIVT have not been viewed as serious athletes.

The formal inclusion of the women's game in the NACIVT did not occur without resistance. While "women demanded that they have the opportunity to compete [...] tradition did not give" ("A short history" 1999, 25). One of the people who played a key role in facilitating women's participation explained that he had to go against the elders of the tournament even to hold an exhibition game (see also "A short history 1999," 25). The details of the resistance were not given in "A Short History"; however, Michael speculated that certain elders could not understand the need to include women's teams and were less interested in being inclusive than in just playing volleyball. Nick agreed, and reasoned that "the older generation, the *purists*, they just want to play" and were therefore not committed to inclusion. According to these two interviewees, it seems that there was a view that the women's division would be a distraction or that players and organizers at that time were not concerned with increasing participation, inclusion, or fairness. They just wanted to play volleyball. Furthermore, it may be that volleyball (or perhaps sport in general) was seen as a male domain, a view that is certainly not unique to the "elders" or to Chinese men at the time. On the other hand, where the presence of women was acceptable and even welcomed was on the sidelines as girl-friends or wives of players. Early in the 2015 practice season for one men's team in Toronto, there was a "group of girls ... three or four of them who would go every single weekend and [...] literally just sit in the gym and watch them practice" (Wendy). At a team practice, I too saw a number of girlfriends, some of them players on a team for a different club, watching their partners practice. Women are welcomed as fans and supporters; but as players, it is clear that women athletes and the women's game are constructed in ways that reinforce their subordinate position.

Historically, for example, women players were seen as a distraction or even a disruptive presence in the tournament. One retired player who played a few decades ago stated that he

hated the girls' teams. Everywhere you travel with them, they take so long to put the make up on. You got to wait for them for dinner ... I said, next year no more girls' team, we're gonna be late for dinner, late for the plane (laughs).

While this interviewee was trying to make a joke, his humour also serves as an alibi for stereotypes about women and femininity. The assumption that the women's teams would get in the way of the *real* focus of the tournament (i.e., volleyball) and would be disruptive by delaying other teams because they were busy putting on makeup suggests that women players are not serious, competitive athletes. Such perceptions are surely not confined to the elders or other male members of the NACIVT who resisted the inclusion of women in the sport (e.g., Hess 2000; Laurendeau & Sharara 2008; Theberge 1994).

Decades later, this opinion that women athletes and the women's division are troublesome persists. For example, when asked what challenges there have been in the NACIVT over the years, one former player explained that the women's teams are "more catty" and that they are more likely to lodge protests with regard to the eligibility rules or to resist changes to the rules. He pointed to the women's Captains' Meeting as evidence, stating that their meetings last much longer (Field Notes, Washington Tournament). Later, he pointed out that the women are more cautious about any changes to the eligibility rules because they only have six players on the court, and any changes could impact them far more than they would affect a nine-man team, which has more players, suggesting that their concerns might be reasonable and justified.

Another older alumni player reiterated the position that women players were more difficult. He recalled that "it's only the women [who argue about the rule]. Always the women. [...] We [the men] never have that problem [...] the women object to everything." Upon hearing this observation, a former player, now a coach, proclaimed, "I didn't know it had to do with the women's division. So it was the women who started it all!" thereby placing the blame for conflicts in the tournament solely on shoulders of the women players. Whereas in the men's game, raising a challenge about the eligibility of players on an opposing team is sometimes viewed as a strategy to increase the chances of winning, in the case of the women, such a move is interpreted in a reductive way, suggesting that it is because of their maliciousness, rather than a desire for fair competition stemming from their identities as serious athletes.

Actually, in some instances, women players were not seen as athletes and dedicated volleyball players. For example, Michael explained that before the women's division started "we had young kids like him [pointing to a now retired player] at that time, that start[ed] playing. The girls follow them *of course*" (emphasis added). What is interesting about this assertion is that Michael concluded that the girls attended the matches to watch the men play "of course," rather than speculating that they were sports fans. The sense of the women not being seen as serious athletes was also reflected in a comment about the team names. Ken (64 years old, second generation) explained how certain (men's) teams have historic Chinese names and expressed regret that some teams had chosen to change names. He then stated that "women's teams are more pick up; they just pull a name out of a hat." This statement unfairly characterizes women's teams, especially since a number of them have been together and competing in the tournament for more than a decade.

The play of individual women and their athleticism could also be framed in gendered but sometimes transformative ways. For example, a spectator was overheard observing that "the girls are so much more gentle than what I'm used to" (Field Notes, Washington Tournament). She was a parent of one of the players from the men's team of the same club. This perception reinforces the view that women athletes are not as strong and aggressive and play in a much more subdued way. While such interpretations are common (e.g., Elueze & Jones 1998; Halbert & Latimer 1994; Pirinen 1997), I also overheard the opposite commentary during another tournament. During a women's match at the Toronto tournament, two male players admired a woman who had just made a powerful spike. They marvelled at the strength and speed that she generated. This player's reputation was known to the two observers, and they proceeded to praise her success in international beach volleyball competitions. During our interview, Patrick (33 years old, second generation) also expressed admiration for the strength and power of women players in the NACIVT (June 2015). These examples illustrate how gendered views of women's passivity and transformative interpretations of women's strength exist simultaneously within the NACIVT.

Related to the devaluing of women's athleticism is the undercurrent of sexualizing women, something that is common in sports more broadly, as feminist scholars have pointed out (e.g., Birrell & Theberge 1994; Choi 2000; Hall 1996; Holmlund 1994; Messner 2002; Schultz 2005). For example, on the first day of the Toronto tournament, I came across an old friend who was competing in the men's division. After exchanging pleasantries, I asked him why he joined the NACIVT team and he joked that it was "to pick up chicks." A similar comment was shared by Christie who recalled when her brother and his friends came to see the tournament for the first time. She stated that one of her brother's friends "likes Asian women, so he's like 'This is awesome, why didn't you tell me, Christie? I could meet chicks here!'" When she shared the story, she looked exasperated, as though this was not the first time that she had heard these types of comments.

The most obvious example of the sexualizing of women occurred during an initiation ritual at one of the tournament banquets. In recent years, the initiations had become "a little risqué and sexual" (an alumnus). An alumnus player admitted that the initiations were getting out of hand and recalled an example where two young women had to remove their bras on stage during the tournament. He seemed to think that "they love it" and laughed as he recounted this incident. That women's bodies and sexuality are used as a form of entertainment further illustrates how women players are perceived within the tournament. They are not fellow athletes whose hard work, training, and athleticism should be celebrated but instead are sources of shame (via hazing) and entertainment via a masculinist gaze.

In contrast to this explicit display of sexuality and objectification of women through hazing rituals, one former participant recalled an attempt to control women's behaviour and contain their sexuality. Specifically, she and her teammates were reminded that they were representing the entire volleyball club and that if other players "see a whole bunch of wild sixteen-, seventeen-year-olds boozing it up, dancing with every single guy, it's going to look bad on our club." Her group of friends were seen as particularly troublesome because "we wanted to like have fun and go out at night and party and be what they would see as stereotypically very North American girls, and that's what we were, and we were seen as different, just a different breed." There is a clear intersection between gender and culture, whereby their performance of gender was viewed as reflecting that of "North American girls" and there-fore inappropriate for "good" "Chinese or Asian girls." Instead, young women on the team were expected to behave "properly," including not drinking excessively and not socializing with "every single guy," because such behaviour would tarnish the reputation of the club. Thus, women's decorum and sexuality came to reflect the honour and status of others in the community. This is similar to how the contestants in the Japanese American beauty pageant that King-O'Riain (2006) studied were also tightly controlled and chaperoned so as to protect the image of the event and the organi-zation. This player recalled being self-conscious about interacting with players from other teams because she and her teammates had been lectured about being loyal to the club by only socializing with teammates and other players in the club. She recounted being seen as "too social and almost even promiscuous and that was sort of a bad assumption." Although couched in the language of loyalty to one's club, women's sexuality was being controlled by the implica-tion of promiscuity if she and her teammates were not being faith-ful to their own club. In both instances, women's bodies were seen as the domain of men, either to be consumed for entertainment or to be controlled to reflect authority and honour.

It should be noted that objectification of men did occur. One player described her initial interest in the tournament in terms of her attraction to a player. She recalled thinking "that guy's really hot, I wanna get into this league" (Diane). Another former player and organizer also described how, near the end of her career, the new players who were joining her club were "boy-crazy. Like they're just playing the sport because they know there's all these guys there." It was an approach to the tournament to which she could not relate and that ultimately exacerbated the generation gap she already felt with these players. Men's bodies were also put on display, although in a different way from the strip-tease example given above. A number of male interviewees recalled initiation rituals, for instance, that involved nudity. These rites often took place in public such as in communal spaces of the hotel (e.g., hallways, the lobby, elevators) and also involved power relations, in this case between rookies and senior players. These practices do, however, involve a homoeroticism (Pronger 1992) that may transgress assumptions around "appropriate" masculine behaviour, while at the same time reinforcing them because initiation rites are often linked to the presumption that participation demonstrates brotherhood (johnson & Holman 2004). There was also a subversion of the usual male gaze, as sometimes women's teams of the same club would witness these rituals and the humiliation of male players.

Despite the homoeroticism of these hazing rituals and the occasional shifting gaze and object of consumption, the heteronormative undertones that are linked to gendered assumptions about women athletes are unmistakable. For example, Michael assumed that girls who came to watch the tournament were *obviously* attending as girlfriends and to watch the young men who had begun playing the sport. Another former player noted that there was a time when the men's teams in his club would not have survived had it not been for the women's team; the women often invited their boyfriends to join. Indeed, a member of a club that does not have a women's team indicated that a women's team would help with recruiting players to the men's teams. When coupled with the lower status of the women's game and the assumption that women athletes were a disruptive presence in the NACIVT, it is clear that women players in this case were valued for what they brought into the club via their assumed heterosexuality. Even in the official history of the tournament, women are present only in heteronormative relationships. For instance, the lives of early Chinese immigrants in the United States are described as "all the more difficult to bear for loneliness." There were "nearly three Chinese male[s] for every Chinese female," making it "difficult for a Chinese immigrant to start a family" ("A short history" 1999, 22). Such statements simultaneously reinforce heteronormativity and limit women's experiences to being mothers and wives.

Furthermore, just as ethnic socializing offered parents of the Japanese American communities studied by Chin (2012, 2016) and King-O'Riain (2006) the hope that their children would find a heterosexual ethnic partner, so too did the NACIVT serve as a site for heterosexual matchmaking. For example, one former player recalled that during his time, "because of the girls and guys, there's so many [matches] … it's a matchmaker. It's a lot of, a matchmaker. Yeah. I mean they met on the court! And they marry!" Heterosexuality was and continued to be an assumed norm within the tournament. As Kyle stated, "The younger guys are going down, there's girls, and they wanna see girls, they wanna go party with different girls from different cities and hook up. So, yeah, it definitely happens." Similarly, Mark claimed that "*every* young guy's *always* like 'Oh, yeah, there's a team of girls right there.' *Of course* it's [interest in women's teams] going to be there" (emphasis added). Thus, both presume that there is a common desire among the young men for women players and that heterosexuality is the norm. Even when the assumption that men participate for the opportunity to meet women is minimized, heteronormativity and the objectification of women continue to operate. As one interviewee stated, the presence of women for the men is "just a bonus […] just gravy." There are a number of other examples where heterosexuality is presumed. In a comment of 21 August 2001 in the guest book from nacivt.com, for example, one writer states that a certain men's junior team could improve if "they get their act together (stop thinking about girls)" (*NACIVT.com guestbook*, n.d.). Female players are presumed to be interested in male players and vice versa (e.g., Karen; Dow 1978, as cited in "62nd Tournament booklet" 2006, 61).

The subordinate status of women in the NACIVT is also reflected in the comparative absence of women in positions of power and influence within the NACIVT. For example, according to the 60th tournament website, the officers and lifetime directors of the North American Chinese Volleyball Association – Boston Chapter are all men. This imbalance may be in part because, as noted above, women did not begin participating in the tournament until forty years ago. However, some current elders started playing around that time, making it plausible that women might also have been eligible to be part of this group of respected and influential alumni. Nonetheless, in the interviews I conducted and in all the texts I analysed during my research, only one woman from San Francisco was mentioned as a highly respected organizer. Even after she passed away, tournaments are still held in her honour. Perhaps in part because positions of power and influence were held by men, "old men" were cited as the reason for the lack of change within the tournament and with respect to the eligibility rules.

Women do hold positions of power on organizing committees – for example, as the chairs of the Toronto and San Francisco tournament committees (e.g., 2005, 2007, 2012, 2014). Furthermore, the NACIVT governing committee that is formed for each tournament is made up of a male and female representative from each city. Nevertheless, since these groups are disbanded after each tournament, it is difficult to suggest that there is gender parity in decision-making power. The lack of influence of women players was exemplified by the interviewees' introduction to the NACIVT. A number of male players were inspired to join the tournament through male relatives, such that a clear fraternal line of participation could clearly be traced. Women, on the other hand, were usually recruited or invited by friends; only one interviewee indicated being influenced by a family member, but again, this was a male relative.

The lack of women in positions of power was also reflected in the gendered delegation of responsibilities. For example, during the Toronto tournament, I observed middle-aged women taking care of the food needs of teams. One woman at the Washington tournament even described her role as "the mother hen" for one junior team. There were also other women in attendance because their adolescent children played. Some of these women were former players. Interestingly, I met a handful of fathers who continue to play or remain involved as coaches. Mothers, on the other hand, were less likely to continue playing, though one woman did coach a junior team. Instead, women who used to play were more likely to "come back as mothers [and watch], 'cause their children play" (Ken). In such instances, the women could garner the respect of the players, even within the constrained role of wife or mother. At one long-established Toronto club, one mother attended every practice and every tournament, taking statistics of players' performances and supporting her son's team. Although her constant presence subsequently led players to tease her son for being a "mama's boy," thereby reproducing notions of what is expected of a "man," she was also respected for her commitment to the club.

The status of women and of the women's game within the NACIVT is in striking contrast to the findings of Willms and Chin, who both examine the Japanese American basketball leagues in Los Angeles, California. Willms (2010) is interested in how these "J-Leagues" organize and understand themselves in relation to hegemonic operations of race, ethnicity, and gender. She found that there is a unique gender regime operating within these leagues because girls' and women's participation and especially their success in basketball, both within the league and beyond, are critical to maintaining community and building a sense of identity in relation to stereotypes of Asian athleticism. This is similar to the findings of Chin (2012), who looked at Japanese American youth basketball leagues and their meaning and significance for ethnic identity and community building. She observed that the league and the community celebrated highly skilled girls and women athletes in the league, and that they served as a resource for galvanizing ethnic solidarity in a way that the boys and men could not. Interestingly, Yep (2009) reaches similar conclusions about the Chinese American women who played basketball in San Francisco in the 1930s and 1940s, stating that the "mostly working-class Chinese American women used their athletic bodies to create community" (63) and became role models for younger people in Chinatown, irrespective of gender. The differences in the findings of the present study from the previous literature are likely related to the higher status of men as athletes and that of the nine-man game.

The perception of women players as less serious athletes or of the women's game as more informal is reflected in the difference in status between the men's and women's games during the annual

Labour Day Tournament. At the 2005 tournament held in Toronto, both the men's and women's finals were occurring simultaneously. The court where the men's match was held was surrounded by spectators. In fact, most people were sitting or standing by the court long before the game began, in order to ensure that they had a prime location from which to watch. In comparison, the women's final had very few people watching. So sparse were the spectators that those standing on the fringes of the men's game, could simply turn around and watch the women's match because, despite the distance, their view would not be obstructed by fans. It was only after the men's final had finished that many, though not all, spectators then moved to watch the women's match (Field Notes, Toronto Tournament).

Adam, a former player and organizer agreed that the men's game attracted far more spectators than the women's game. He explained that efforts have been made to stagger the schedule so that both matches do not occur at the same time. However, should both finals be taking place simultaneously, "everyone's gonna watch the men's game and not the women's game" (Adam). This was reiterated by another player who (on 10 September 2002) wrote in the guestbook of the former nacivt.com website that "people focus way too much on 9-men and neglect the women's games […] 99% of the people supported the guys' final rather than the women's" (*NACIVT.com guestbook*, n.d.). On the same date a participant from Boston immediately concurred, suggesting that this had always been the case: "At all the NACIVT tournaments of the MINIS, all the focus [has] always been with the 9-men, I guess 'cause it's something different compared to the usual 6-men games," which is what the women play (*NACIVT.com guestbook*, n.d.). As Irene puts it, "you could ask who won the women's last year and probably very few people would be able to remember. But everybody will know who won the men's tournament." While the crowds have increased for the women's game, "there's still that second-class status that the women do feel" (Lisa) as a result of the continued central place the men's game holds within the NACIVT.

This prominence is demonstrated in other ways. For example, in the seven tournament booklets examined in this study, the pictures that were featured, not including team photos, are mostly those of men's teams or of the men's game. Only one booklet had photos of women playing on the cover ("58th Tournament booklet" 2002). The rest were dominated by images of men playing nine-man. Lisa also made this observation, stating that "most of the things that you do see about the [NACIVT] is just pictures of the men, especially if they're using older photographs. You only see the guys." Furthermore, Lisa blamed the common reference of calling "Chinese volleyball" *"nine-man"* and how this creates an assumption that women do not play or that they play nines as well. The irony, of course is that she does not see a problem in calling the NACIVT "Chinese volleyball," despite the presence of other "Asian" people.

The central place of the men's game is also evident in the layout of the tournament site. For example, at the New York Mini tournament in 2006, the men's teams played on a larger, raised tennis court. The men's teams also played on the courts that were closer to the entrance and sidewalk where pedestrians could stop and watch. The courts for the women's games, on the other hand, were on the opposite side, making it impossible for pedestrians to watch. This is in striking contrast to the layout of the courts on the first day of the 2005 Labour Day tournament. The space was divided such that courts for both men's and women's games were given equal prominence. Although the men's games were played directly in front of the entrance where spectators entered, courts for both were located immediately below the gallery that provided a bird's-eye view of matches. Perhaps the most significant example of the prestige of the men's game and the neglect of the women's division was demonstrated at the San Francisco tournament in 2007. The theme of the tournament was to embrace and celebrate the heritage and history of the NACIVT. In keeping with this goal, the organizing committee coordinated a "Classics Game," an exhibition nine-man game that would "feature the stars who have given this game its meaning" (*Classics game* 2007). Retired nines players were invited to register and participate in the game. Certainly, this effort to recognize alumni players is commendable. Unfortunately, the neglect of the women's history and heritage within the NACIVT is conspicuous, particularly since

2007 marked the thirtieth anniversary of the women's division in the NACIVT. Instead, this moment of NACIVT history remained overlooked.

Efforts have been made to ensure that the finals for the women's division championship are given just as much attention as the men's final. For example, Adam recalled how, when he organized the tournament in Toronto, he worked to ensure that the times of the men's and women's finals were staggered. This was also done at the San Francisco tournament in 2007, a move that was appreciated by a participant who (on 7 September 2007) wrote on a message board that "this allowed for the championship game to have a set of spectators that the women's final normally doesn't attract. Kudos for this" (*NACIVT-SF* n.d.). Nevertheless, organizers of the NACIVT and long-time participants who continue to exert influence over the operation of the tournament need to examine how women and the women's game are being constructed in gendered ways. Furthermore, while interviewees mentioned having role models among other players (Sarah, Phoebe), there are clearly not enough positive examples of women in positions of power. One interviewee confessed that he was concerned about the commitment level of young people and, consequently, the sustainability of the tournament in the future. He stated that the "turnover [of players] is high, especially on girls' teams." When asked why, he explained that "they get married and stuff." While this may be true for some women, it is important to examine whether there are structural factors – such as being seen as disruptive and difficult, being sexualized, and not being taken seriously as athletes – that play a role in their shorter careers. Furthermore, as the discussion of the eligibility rules demonstrates, individuals whose playing time is limited experience frustration and are more likely to consider quitting. Dismissing women's experiences as "getting married and stuff" neglects the factors that constrain their participation.

The NACIVT can serve as a site for negotiating gender identities (Y. Lee 2005, 2015) in terms of rejecting "traditional" femininity and exploring different forms of femininity, such as being athletic, strong, and powerful. At the same time, the women are constrained by gendered responsibilities, limited access to positions of power and influence, the assumption that their sexuality is something to be consumed and controlled, and, most significantly, the lack of status of the women's game. It is this lack of status that has implications for understanding the meaning of the eligibility rules and the women's game, and how the threat of "Whiteness" operates via gender.

In her study on Japanese American beauty pageants, King-O'Riain (2006) observed that the question of whether a mixed-race person could represent the Japanese American community as queen reproduced the hierarchy of "Whiteness" as the standard of beauty and femininity. Originally, beauty pageants for the Japanese American community were intended to affirm and celebrate Japanese American women as beautiful because, in the broader sociocultural context, they were not admired and their beauty could not compete in Miss America beauty pageants because they did not reflect dominant beauty norms. In 2014, when Nina Davuluri became the first Indian-American woman to be crowned Miss America, some felt that Miss Kansas, a blonde-haired, blue-eyed "White" woman was more deserving (Hafiz 2013). This negative reaction is indicative of how "Whiteness" is seen to represent America and the definition of beauty. For Japanese American women, having their own beauty pageants serves as a form of resistance against these dominant beauty norms (King-O'Riain 2006). Nonetheless, the rationale for the pageant illustrates how race and biological essentialism remain defining categories through which Japanese American femininity is framed. The pageant – or the story that is told, anyway – illustrates the ongoing belief in race. Mixed-race women are a threat because of the view that Japanese women, being limited by their biologies (stereotypically thought of as "short," "flat-chested," and so on), cannot compete. While King-O'Riain (2006) is referring to being competitive in beauty pageants, the same can be said for the case of Asian women athletes and the threat of Whiteness.

Within a sporting context, a traditionally masculine space, women athletes – even those who are highly successful and accomplished – occupy the margins. In the NACIVT community, where the men's game has a position of prominence and where women are not taken seriously as athletes, sporting Asian women's belonging is tenuous. If they are not players, then they occupy gendered and secondary roles as mothers, wives, and girlfriends. In this instance, the threat of Whiteness operates through the lens of gender not as a threat to traditional femininity (as is the case for Asian men and masculinity) but as a threat to their belonging within the NACIVT as sporting women. The conflicts that arise during women's games with regard to the eligibility rules may be related to the shaky legitimacy of the women's athleticism and the women's game, which in turn is essentialized as slower and less powerful because of the players' gender. This is in turn exacerbated by women's exclusion from the nines game, the main cultural phenomenon that is celebrated and perceived to be protected via eligibility rules. Since women are often seen as the reproducers of culture (King-O'Riain, 2006), the fact that women athletes in the NACIVT do not have an explicit participatory role in the continuation of nine-man emphasizes their tenuous belonging by reconfiguring this relationship between gender and culture.

Culture

Christie was the first mixed-race NACIVT player I interviewed. I was introduced to her through one of her teammates who had already participated in the research. I knew only that she was of mixed-race background. In light of the eligibility rules, I was keen to hear her story, my anticipation reflecting an assumption that she would be quite critical of these stipulations. Over the course of the interview, Christie made it clear that, throughout her childhood and upbringing, she sought out places to belong and to be accepted by others, both in and outside of the NACIVT. She was protective, therefore, of the sense of belonging that she found via the NACIVT. The belonging that is apparently protected by the eligibility rules is tied together with other emotionally invested ideas like culture, tradition, and – most significantly – authenticity that are especially meaningful for those who are read as Other because of their mixed-race background. Thus, for Christie, as someone already on the margins, the eligibility rules were a complex and difficult issue.

When asked "What would happen if the tournament was opened to everybody?" Christie responded,

> It would become ... the Asian culture would totally phase out and it would be diluted with many, many, many good Caucasian, and Black and Hispanic, all different races, coming into play, mostly White. And yeah, it would be nice to open up the tournament to more people because it would make it a bigger tournament and it would have hundreds of more participants. But it would mean that special closeness and the inspirational side of Asian culture that we really hold on to ... I don't think any, even half-Asians or Japanese or Korean or anyone who was not full Chinese, I don't ... many may say, some of them might say "Yeah, let's open it up to any culture," but I think in the end that everyone would say "No, let's keep it Asian, let's keep it something that we can hold on to as a culturally developing athletic association."

Christie's comment illustrates how the presence of "Caucasian, Black and Hispanic, all different races" of people would threaten the "purity" and potency of Asian culture and its continued presence within the NACIVT. The viability of Asian culture, then, depended on Asian bodies. Furthermore, she was fairly confident that everyone would agree with her view to keep the NACIVT entirely Asian, for as she implies, there is a closeness entailed by Asianness that would be undone if the tournament were open to all. There is an assumption of primordial unity among all Asians that provides this "special closeness," in part because Asians are equally inspired by "Asian culture." Thus, just as biological essentialism served as justification for the eligibility rules, so too is identity essentialized, such that culture and cultural knowledge are seen to be housed within the bodies of Asian people. Asian culture is taken as given, uniting a diverse but nevertheless similar group of people. Furthermore, the sense of intimacy and familiarity that is supposedly shared among Asian people remains unquestioned.

Asianness served as a unifying umbrella term, one that served to include all participants and involve them in the project of maintaining its boundaries. In other words, the idea of shared Asianness functioned to unite and erase differences. For example, Nancy explained that the goal of the tournament is to honour and maintain "a heritage from China." She goes on to state that if rules regarding ethnicity and eligibility were abolished, then

> it's not the Asian tradition and it kinda, it kinda contradicts the whole nine-man because the only reason ... it started with nine-man right, and of course it's an Asian tradition, that's the nine-man. [...] if we open it to just anybody could play, [...] it's going to decrease its appeal to the Asian community.

Like Nancy, Christie also uses "Chinese" and "Asian" interchangeably. For instance, when asked about her views about playing in or outside of Chinatown, she seemed to think that it does not matter where she plays because "culturally, you're still around all these Asians so it's still there [even if you do not play in Chinatown]." The Chinese cultural element that playing in Chinatown is thought to provide is located within the bodies of Asian athletes who surround her when she is playing.

The blurring of Chineseness and Asianness was particularly evident in how the interviewees described the tournament and certain practices. For example, Rob stated that

> Asianness and all that really does come into play and there's a lot of traditions involved, the bowing before and at the end of a game. Just the rules, everything. It's meant to help protect and preserve and perpetuate a certain ... cultural group's kind of symbols and rituals and it's overt.

While he refers to the traditions as Asianness, the group that is being protected, preserved, and perpetuated through the eligibility rules is "100 per cent Chinese," since it is the group that is given full status in the tournament and can play the majority of the time. Similarly, in describing how the tournament organizing committee negotiated relationships with the Chinatown business community, one of the organizers explained that representatives from Chinatown were given the head title.

As Adam explained, "In Asian culture, Chinese culture, there's a lot of face so you wanna make sure that you're giving them the respect that everything's fine, the façade is there, it's pristine." He noted as well that when dignitaries such as the Consul General of China attended the banquet, it was important to acknowledge their presence and their support and stated that "again that whole Asian thing about the face, it's important, you *have* to show them respect, you *have* to make them seem important, even though you know in your heart of hearts that, yeah ... they're just there." Thus, even in referring to cultural practices and beliefs, interviewees used Asian and Chinese in inconsistent ways, often blurring the two. And yet, the eligibility rules make it clear that the Chineseness of the NACIVT is critically important to maintain.

Chineseness is presumed to be the connection between culture and the nation – a presumption that renders Chineseness as rooted in China. The greater the geographical and generational distance from China, the greater the feelings of shame resulting from lack of authenticity, inadequacy, and impurity. Such a view of Chinese identity is the result of an "interlocking of [...] mutual discursive exclusionism" (Ang 2001, 32). A second way in which Chinese identity is defined includes the culturalist notion of Chineseness or a feeling of having Chinese cultural heritage. Ang states that this would mean some individuals would not count as Chinese and yet still think of themselves as such, or, conversely, would include those who do not always know themselves as Chinese. Furthermore, this definition perpetuates the struggle for "authentic" culture and can reinforce feelings of guilt or incompetence. The third definition is the notion of being members of a Chinese race. Ang calls this reductionist, since it

constructs the subject as passively and linearly (pre)determined by "blood," not as an active historical agent whose subjectivity is continually shaped through his/her engagements with multiple, complex and contradictory social relations that are over-determined by political, economic, and cultural circumstances in highly particular spatio-temporal contexts. (Ang 2001, 49)

The results of determining Chinese culture, nation, and "blood" as an essential feature of Chinese identity promotes, according to A. Ong (1998), a sense that Chinese people exist in their own separate and distinct worlds and therefore reinforces orientalism, be it self-imposed or in the media.

How Chineseness is defined within the NACIVT is most closely aligned with this third definition, whereby, through the eligibility rules, "Chinese" is defined only as those who are "100 per cent" or, stated more bluntly, of "pure blood." In turn, the Chineseness of the tournament is exemplified by the dominant presence of "100 per cent Chinese" people. For example, James stated that the tournament is "not really Chinese because you're seeing players that are Korean, Filipino, Vietnamese, Laotian," and so on. In other words, if the tournament were populated entirely by Chinese people, it would seem more Chinese, according to James's logic. Similarly, Lisa explained that being "surrounded by a lot more Chinese people" is what sparked her interest in learning more about Chineseness. She also described how she felt when she was first approached to join an NACIVT team as "being recognized by my own people," a recognition that was different from that which she experienced in mainstream regional teams. Unlike the link with Chinatown, access to Chinese food, or speaking a Chinese language – all of which varied in importance – the presence of Chinese people as emblematic of the Chineseness of the tournament did not waver. It was the Chinese people, whose participation was protected by the rules, who provided the Chinese character of the tournament. The rules prevent, as Irene observes, having an entirely Korean team, for example, and ensures Chinese dominance on every team. The Chinese character of the tournament is maintained by the dominant presence of Chinese players on all teams, and the overarching Asianness of the tournament is conferred through the discursive blurring of Chineseness and Asianness.

Implicit in this view is that Chineseness is owned by those who are "100 per cent Chinese." This was most clearly illustrated by the following comment made by a long-time participant who had played with two different teams. He explained that he was born in Hong Kong and therefore has a sense of his Chinese identity:

"I know my history, I know where I came from." In this way, he reproduces what Ang (2001) calls a reductionist definition because it treats the subject as passive and overdetermined by lineage and by nation. In doing so, this participant reinforces orientalism (A. Ong 1998). This participant went onto explain that, by comparison, mixed-race children are "a lost generation," echoing the *juk-sing* pejorative that constructs individuals as neither one nor the other, as in a void or lost (Pon 2000b). Thus, participation in NACIVT is critical for these "lost" individuals so that they too may "feel a sense of pride through participation." This player – given his "100 per cent" status – demonstrates confidence and security in his ownership and knowledge of Chineseness based on place of birth, and also, by implication, in his assessment of mixed-race children as "lost." Children of mixed-race background are "lost" because they are not well-versed in their history and their origins. He later remarked that they "act White or Black" rather than appropriately "Chinese." This player thus reproduced the trope of purity and impurity and the conflation of race and ethnicity whereby race confers ethnic membership.

This stands in stark contrast to Christie's experience. Christie, someone whom the previous interviewee would consider "lost," bitterly recounted how people think she's White, and yet she is the one who is trying to uphold Asian values. She recalled how disappointed she was to learn of the sexually explicit behaviour of younger players during the tournament banquet. The players had been separated into two different banquet sites, and she learned that at the other banquet, some of the women did a striptease on stage in front of their peers as part of the initiation of rookie players. Christie was "disgusted" and "really pissed off." Her disappointment was closely connected to what she saw as a disregard for Asian values:

> I was taught straight off, right in the beginning that being in Asian culture, you have to respect one another, and respect your roots and respect the people who were here before you and then to treat it trashy [by behaving inappropriately]? And I'm just this halfie girl that everyone calls White on the court, like "[Christie's] White" and I'm the one being

like "Show your respect, this is disrespectful and you're putting shame to a lot of people not just yourself but to other players."

Christie is cognizant of being seen as not completely Chinese, to the point that she is removed from the category entirely and deemed to be White.[1] In turn, she illustrates her Asianness and her ethnic legitimacy (Root 2002) not by pointing out her Chinese heritage but by practising Asian cultural values. This experience is similar to that of her half-Chinese teammate who, when mistreated in Chinese restaurants, would berate waiters in fluent Chinese. Like the beauty pageants' participants in King-O'Riain's (2006) study, both Christie and her teammate perform culture in order to claim ethnic membership. While they undoubtedly are resisting the definition of Chineseness that is limited to "100 per cent Chinese" and that conflates race with ethnicity, the fact that they were nonetheless read as "White" suggests that their impact was limited. The view that Chineseness and the claim to Chinese culture were innate in the bodies of "100 per cent" or pure Chinese people was already institutionalized within the eligibility rules and enacted in how they were read and treated.

I do not wish to dismiss the significance of the cultural connection to the NACIVT. Through the NACIVT, many interviewees discovered, learned about, and were able to lay claim to a culture (chapter 4). NACIVT is a significant forum for engaging in meaningful cultural practices, and was especially so in its early form when most Chinese migrants did not have families and had limited opportunities for socializing because of financial and time constraints. However, when culture is essentialized and is given as the rationale for boundaries, the notion of culture is not examined. For example, when asked how he responds to accusations of racism, Steve replied, "I always answer back saying it's a cultural event that allowed us to keep our culture intact. Just like fraternities would." Implicit in this statement is the importance of keeping culture unchanged and uncontaminated by the incursion of

---

1 This is similar to another player who, as noted previously, was referred to as "White boy" or "White man" by his coach.

Others. Further, Steve undoubtedly assumes culture to be a homogeneous, uniform entity, not one that is the culmination of interaction with diversity or that is constructed through travel and at the intersection of routes and roots (Clifford 1997). Both Rob and Lisa held similar views to Steve's, with Lisa succinctly explaining that the eligibility rules are "the only way to preserve the culture of the game." Since the eligibility rules privilege those who are "100 per cent Chinese," the ideas of culture and "pure" Chinese stay interconnected, and the need to protect them remains unquestioned. It is not culture that is being protected through exclusion but exclusion that is being maintained and boundaries justified by defining culture in strategic, essentializing ways.

Essentializing Biology and Identity

Edwards (2001) states that in using diaspora we need to keep "room for ideological difference and disjuncture" (50) as well as be flexible, spanning both space and time. He introduces the concept of *décalage* in his attempt to address the internal differences of diaspora. These differences are a "residue, perhaps of what resists translation or what sometimes cannot help refusing translation across the boundaries of language, class, gender, sexuality, religion, the nation-state" (64). Using this as a departure point is to undertake "the reestablishment of a prior unevenness or diversity" (65). It means asking what props, or what Edwards calls "*calé,*" create the stable sense of belonging in NACIVT. What happens when those props are jostled, and what discursive work is done to restabilize the diaspora and maintain its constructed stability? The concept of *décalage* helps to illustrate how linkages are sustained through difference, as well as how difference can be continually marginalized and erased in order to maintain the fixity and stability of the community. By simultaneously holding together the overcoming and erasure of difference, *décalage* allows for approaching with compassion attempts to build community ties while at the same time illustrating how these efforts function in ways that can render invisible the very gap that must be crossed to build bridges.

To use diaspora theoretically and methodologically in this way, then, is to centre difference and to consider how linkages are made through and across difference, or how the collective "we" is produced (Brah 1996) in relation to these differences. In the case of the NACIVT, difference was understood in essentializing ways, as illustrated through participants' views on Whiteness, Asianness, Chineseness, gender, and culture.

A key way in which exclusion of difference was justified was through biological essentialism that operated via race and gender. Whiteness, in terms of perceived greater height and athleticism and the sociohistorical context of volleyball, was named as particularly threatening to the integrity of the community being cultivated via the NACIVT and protected by the eligibility rules. Notions of race served primarily to mark and police the boundaries of Asian and non-Asian in that the interviewees and the larger NACIVT community relied on racialized and essentialized definitions of who and what is Asian. In the NACIVT, the assumption of sameness, particularly around athletic ability, forms the foundation upon which boundaries are justified. Asianness was understood via biological racism, and thus Asian bodies were constructed as shorter and less powerful than White bodies. Despite the prevalence of players who did not fit the stereotype and observation by one interviewee that the NACIVT was a collection of very tall Asian people, this assumption of shorter stature and subsequent limits on playing ability and opportunity necessitated and justified the tournament and the boundaries that dictated eligibility. Racializing Asianness therefore simultaneously warrants the need for an Asian-only space and reinforces biological racism in a cyclical fashion. It can also serve to support racist discourses of lack of athleticism and Asian frailty.

The biological essentialism that framed the interviewees' understanding of Asianness and Whiteness was also manifested in discussions of the men's versus the women's game of volleyball. Interestingly, similar ideas of the superior height and athleticism of men were used to justify why women are relegated to sixes rather than the prestigious nine-man game. These ideas, when coupled with gendered notions of women's lack of recognition as "real" athletes and heteronormative explanations framing their sports participation as an activity that ends with marriage and motherhood, work to construct the heterosexual male as the "real" athlete. Biological essentialism therefore operates to reproduce narrow ideas of race and gender within the NACIVT and serves as a key way in which the collective "we" is produced. In other words, it serves as the *calé* or the prop that stabilizes community in relation to difference. Furthermore, this discourse of biological essentialism does not operate alone but alongside the *calé* of essentializing culture to justify the boundaries of community and in turn stabilize a socially constructed community.

Thus, racialization within the NACIVT operated in two ways. First, it structured the terms of belonging because Chinese men were historically excluded from entering mainstream physical activity and recreational spaces. This in turn resulted in organizing games and the tournament outdoors in the streets of Chinatown. Such exclusion continues in the form of rendering all Asians as uninterested in, incapable of, or inept at sports and therefore constructed outside of sporting realms in general and mainstream volleyball teams more specifically. Second, racialization operated within the NACIVT by structuring how Asianness was called upon. The conditions of Asianness or membership were based upon racialized assumptions of homogeneity, purity, and biological racism. Furthermore, essentialized understandings of gender and culture, while ensuring and protecting a sense of community and belonging, also excluded and hierarchized difference. In other words, despite being a reaction to exclusion from mainstream sport, the NACIVT does not escape the circumstances that frame this marginalization; rather, the circumstances partly determine belonging within the NACIVT itself, such that multiracial Asian people are read as "halfies," "White," or "Black, Black, Black" and therefore reproduce the racial and gendered terrain.

Similarly, Thangaraj (2013, 2015a, 2015b), in his work on ethnically exclusive basketball spaces, found that the men in his study perform and claim a masculinity that is constructed in opposition to femininity and in relation to middle-class respectability. He found that the men "perform sporting masculinity with the same categories that originally dislocated them from American-ness" (Thangaraj 2015a, 203). In doing so, they do not dismantle or even critique the intersecting categories of oppression that marginalize them in the first place. Thangaraj, though, writes about these men with tremendous sensitivity, recognizing that the men occupy contradictory positions and that their experience is not simply reproducing hegemonic masculinity at the expense of Others. Indeed, the masculinity they claim is not valued by their own ethnic community, nor is it transferrable beyond the ethnically exclusive sports spaces they created. Moreover, it is evident that these men, despite their athletic prowess, have been subjected to marginalizing experiences such as racist taunting, particularly after 9/11.

Thangaraj's (2013, 2015a, 2015b) work serves as an important reminder and example of criticisms of Othering processes and also of sensitivity to how they may be influenced by sociohistorical structures. Certainly, the importance of breaking down stereotypes of Asian volleyball players as too short and therefore not good enough to play should not be underestimated. The NACIVT provides a highly competitive, skilled level of play, as well as a learning environment for players who may not have been given the opportunity to receive excellent coaching on mainstream teams. In doing so, it enables players' skills to be nurtured, practised, and honed to the point that these athletes are recognized, admired, and recruited by mainstream volleyball players and teams. Thus, the eligibility rules act to ensure that these important volleyball opportunities for Asian players are protected. Should the rules be abolished, in light of the increasingly competitive nature of the tournament and the quest to win the championship, teams may be less inclined to invest the time and energy required to develop the skills of shorter players and more inclined to recruit tall individuals who do not need as much coaching to learn how to "maximize their vertical." Nevertheless, the justification for the eligibility rules, as well as how they are perceived, reinforces biological essentialism related to both Asianness and Whiteness.

Biological essentialism converged with the essentializing of cultural identity in the experience of mixed-race Asian/White players and how they were perceived within the NACIVT. The assumption that Asianness was bounded and unpolluted provided a rationale for the steps taken to protect its supposed purity and prevent possible contamination from Others. Mixing of culture was framed as a threat to the potency of Asianness, and considerable effort was made, and continues to be made, to ensure that Chineseness and Asianness were and are maintained and protected within the NACIVT. This is particularly evident in the rules that limit participation of "non-Asians" within the tournament. Because culture is interpreted as being imprinted upon and owned by Asian bodies, a logic operates to presume that keeping non-Asian bodies out will preserve the coherence and potency of Asian culture. This view necessarily assumes that Asian people are the vessels of Asian culture.

Likewise, Chineseness was presumed to be an eternal entity that was housed in the bodies of Chinese people, despite the multiple ways in which it was being defined, such as originating from China, being able to speak Chinese, and having a Chinese bloodline. The tournament and especially the nine-man game were thought to be unquestionably pure examples of Chinese tradition and culture. That these examples of cultural production and knowledge were a result of movement, travel, and interaction in shifting contact zones is never acknowledged beyond the assumed transfer of this cultural form by migrating Chinese people. In general, Chineseness was viewed as stable based on the assumption of cultural purity and of an unbroken line of ownership between Chinese people and Chinese culture.

Thus, the requirement for a minimum of two-thirds of players to be Chinese is seen to ensure the Chineseness of the tournament. Furthermore, by mandating that each team has a majority of Chinese players on the court, the NACIVT also guarantees the Chineseness of each team. In this way, the eligibility rules maintain the Chineseness of the tournament. The principle works on the assumption that Chinese bodies equal Chineseness. The exclusionary impact of such fixing of categories is made most evident in the unstable place of "half-Chinese" people in the tournament. They are expelled from the category entirely and not permitted to "count" as Chinese persons in the tournament or to enjoy any of the advantages that membership would entail.

These expressions and understandings of "Chineseness" are based on assumptions of stability, purity, and permanence. Thus, they reinforce orientalizing, racist discourses that rely on such notions of fixity and eternalness. This stability of culture is reinforced by the narrative of continuity within NACIVT lore and the importance of volleyball in bridging generational gaps (chapter 4). These racist discourses also serve to exclude and marginalize those who do not fit perfectly into the confines of Chineseness. Ironically, many of the interviewees in this study would no longer qualify as "purely" Chinese because of their migration, their lack of language skill, the fact of their being raised outside of the homeland, and so on. Their claim of belonging, then, is actively produced through new traditions and connections (chapter 4).

Photo 3.1 Toronto Flying Tigers, 1984, location unknown. A left side player passes the ball. Credit: Walter Low.

Photo 3.2 Montreal Freemasons and New York Strangers, 2018, New York. A New York Strangers player attacks. A Montreal Freemasons player is challenging with a block. Credit: Rosanna U.

Photo 3.3 Toronto Ngun Lam and PHI CIA, 2018, New York. A right side wing hit by a Ngun Lam player. Two Philadelphia CIA players block. Credit: Rosanna U.

Chapter 4

Traditions of Continuity and Change

After having talked about the NACIVT for more than an hour, a former NACIVT player offered to show me some tournament-related photos and memorabilia he had collected over the years. We had been sitting at his kitchen table, and he pointed to the door leading to the basement stairs. I followed him down the narrow staircase to find his home office, with one area entirely devoted to his memories of the NACIVT. Pride of place was given to three large photos on display on the wall immediately opposite the stairs. The three photos had each been blown up to the size of a large poster. Each image was framed in thick, dark wood and had a matting to highlight the images. The photos depicted the members of his family, of different generations, who had played in the NACIVT. They were action shots, photos taken while the men were playing. It was clear that the interviewee was particularly proud of the long-standing connection between the NACIVT and his family. The photos and the gallery style in which they were displayed illustrated a tradition of playing volleyball in this particular family, and solidified their membership in a community, although this interviewee's and his father's membership within the NACIVT would never have been questioned. They were after all, 100 per cent Chinese. But what of his son and others who are not? What of players whose families do not have this pedigree, or are of a different immigrant generation, or speak a different language, or speak only English? What of such differences as age, experience, ethnicity, and identity? Once players have passed the criteria for eligibility and entered through the gates of membership, how are differences reconciled in the production of a stable and unified community?

There are a number of differences within the NACIVT that are resolved in the making of community. These differences include but are not limited to generation, age, and position within team hierarchies that together can result in diverse philosophies and priorities. The strategy for producing community in these instances is to put an emphasis on continuity and the passing down of culture, tradition, and knowledge from one generation to the next. According to critics of Asian American research such as Lowe (1996),this approach or vertical axis is a common focus in the study of relationships among Asian Americans (e.g., Chun 2000; Takaki 1989). For example, the relationship between generations, different degrees of assimilation, the role of the second generation in providing a cultural and linguistic link for the first generation, and the passing of cultural knowledge from one generation to the next are but a few ways in which a vertical lens presumes that the unit of analysis is that of generation. Chun (2000) describes the experiences of American-born Chinese as being "a bridge between the parental community and society at large[;] they acted as political representatives, translators, ethnographers, cultural advance guards and entertainers staging Chinese American culture and identity for the broader public" (2). While this position between their parents' generation and American society may have allowed them to "carve out new opportunities for themselves" (2), the primacy of the relationship between parents and children, the vertical lens, and "generation" as the unit of analysis remain intact.

The generational or vertical approach is also commonly used in the study of Asians' participation in sports and physical activity. Often this work shares stories of conflict with parents over sports participation. For example, a study of Korean American women and their sports experiences found that intergenerational conflict was common, particularly around the belief that femininity could be at risk because of involvement in sports (Y. Lee 2005). This issue is not unique to Korean American women, however, and yet because Lee's interviewees are immigrants, it is framed as being an intergenerational conflict. Likewise, Wong's (1999) personal narrative of her experiences as an Asian woman in the United States and her pursuit of sports places an emphasis on clashes with her parents and fails to examine relationships with her peers. She repeatedly points to her parents' values and emphasis on math and science and their lack of appreciation and understanding of sports participation or her desire to pursue a career in physical education (see also Nakamura 2004). Regalado (1992, 2000) also reproduces the prominence of vertical ties at the expense of horizontal connections by organizing his analysis by generation, using *Issei* and *Nisei*, or first and second generation, to describe the place of baseball and other sports in the lives of Japanese Americans. This is not to say that these relationships are not important, but they certainly do not provide a complete picture, particularly since Regalado (2000), in his discussion of sports during the World War Two internment, alludes to the agency and organizational skills of Japanese American *Nisei* women in coordinating sports opportunities for themselves.

In the case of the NACIVT, vertical relationships remain important through the value placed on the passing of traditions from one generation to the next and on overcoming generational differences. This focus on generation is gendered and reproduces the assumption that culture is something whole, pure, and contained. Furthermore, the emphasis on passing down cultural knowledge from one generation to the next, by using the language of "tradition," creates a circular argument for the ongoing justification of the eligibility rules and the Othering of women or mixed-race individuals. That is, the status quo is maintained both through passing down a tradition and through the tradition of passing culture from one generation to the next along vertical relationships. Nonetheless, the new traditions and connections cultivated by the NACIVT participants also illustrate how community is produced through lateral and horizontal relationships and through practices that are specific to the sporting context. These new practices and relationships do not try to erase difference by emphasizing sameness and continuity but instead arise as a result of the increasing diversity of the NACIVT community. These vertical and horizontal relationships intersect and culminate in the role of Chinatown in producing a sense of community among players in NACIVT teams across Canada and the United States.

From One Generation to the Next

"Generation" served as a key construct through which interviewees understood their participation and framed their relationships within the NACIVT. Steve, for example, explained that while he had played on regional, intercollegiate, and even national teams, playing in the NACIVT was different because

> we as Chinese volleyball players are trying to carry on a dynasty, a tradition, if you will. Our forefathers came here, brought this event to keep us together. And you want to fulfil that. I mean, winning's still important of course to me. The reason why I still participate to this day is for this reason, these are my roots and I will always remember that.

In addition, one supporter claimed that the tournament organizers were "a link between the paper sons and the American-born Chinese,"[1] and the tournament was a way to "honor our forefathers" (55th Tournament booklet 1999, 21). Kyle and Nancy, both of whom describe the game as being rooted in China and brought to North America, echoed this connection to origins. For example, Nancy explained that the tournament is "a heritage from China that we're just trying to honour and continue the tradition, and that's the reason why we keep it the way it is. It originated from China, and that's why we continue it." The oft-repeated story of how nine-man volleyball came to be played by Chinese immigrants

---

1 According to US law during the period of Chinese exclusion, if an American fathered a child overseas, the child was an American citizen who was now eligible to enter the United States. During a sojourn back to China, a Chinese labourer who was an American citizen would announce the birth of a child, usually a son, whether or not a birth had taken place. In this way, a "slot" was created that could be sold to another Chinese person who wished to emigrate to the United States despite Chinese exclusion laws. These "fictitious offspring, entering the United States under surnames not their own, were called 'paper sons'" (Pan 1990, 108).

reinforces this sense of uninterrupted linearity, beginning with the invention of volleyball in the United States, its travel to Asia, and its return to Chinatowns in the United States. This journey reflects a supposedly unbroken line between China and Chinatown, affirming the naturalness of the NACIVT players' involvement in this cultural event.

Older family members played an important role in introducing young people to a team and to the tournament. Steve and Nick were just a few of the players who indicated that their fathers, older brothers, and male cousins played in the tournament and that they were inspired by them to play as well (see also N. Lew 2007; R. Lew 2007). Owen recalled that his "friend's father used to play, many many years. So that's why his kids were playing at an early age," implying that this vertical continuity of participation was "natural." This continuity could be seen throughout various clubs in the tournament, where two, even three generations of a family had been involved in the tournament. In one family, a father, his sons, and now his grandson had all been and/or were currently active members on the circuit. Even beyond participation, the head of one long-established team explained to me that he had "inherited the legacy" of his father, who had founded the club, and thus remains heavily involved in the club despite no longer being an active player.

It was a source of pride when this continuity was seen in one family, with generations of players participating in the tournament, as illustrated in the opening anecdote. One player from a US city, a father who continues to play on a team, was overheard proudly introducing his two sons to a friend and indicating that they too were playing in the tournament in the same club. I also observed Ken pointing out a young player to a bystander at a tournament: "This guy here [pointing to a younger player]. I played with his dad, so it continues with each generation." Another player, who submitted his story to the San Francisco tournament website, shared how he, his father, his older brother, his cousin, and now his son play the game: "Looks like tradition continues to carry on throughout the generations" (N. Lew 2007). Similarly, in an article highlighting the career of one player from Washington, the author notes that this player introduced all five of his sons to the tournament: "richly steeped in tradition, bound from generation to generation, [...] he has passed on a tradition of [...] Chinese volleyball for decades to come" (57th Tournament booklet 2001, 39). One woman who used to play now supports her daughter's team. She explained that she wanted her children "to have the same experiences I did. I want it to open doors for them."

Perhaps because of this participation of generations of families, some players hoped that their children would play as well, such as Owen, who said it was "one of my dreams to play with my kids on the court"; Adam, who wanted his "half-Chinese [daughters ...] to play down the road"; or Christie, who expressed a desire for her future children to participate in the tournament. One coach even hoped that he would someday be able to coach and train the children of his current players. Diane noted that she was often teased about when she would be starting her volleyball family, since her husband was also an NACIVT participant. The involvement of children in the tournament was likely facilitated by their attendance at the event. There were a number of pre-adolescent children at the Toronto and Washington Labour Day tournaments, brought by their parents to support siblings or parents. At the Washington tournament in 2006, children were playing informal games of volleyball while matches were taking place. In one group of small children, approximately six to nine years of age, the older children could be heard explaining to their younger friends, "even if it hits the line it's okay." On the last day of the tournament, I saw one boy climbing up the referee ladder at an empty court, gesturing, and pretending to blow a whistle while he refereed an imaginary game. Even at the practices I attended, the coaches' children were present, one even playing on the developmental team. Interestingly, a retired player who helps manage a prominent club admitted that he was uncertain as to whether he wanted his children to participate. He did not want them to carry the burden he feels to maintain the generational continuity of the club.

The significance of continuity between generations was also demonstrated by the interest in passing on knowledge and specific skills to younger players. One retired player said he remained involved because he wanted to share with younger players the knowledge that he had gained. Vic, who began playing nine-man with a local team when he immigrated in his mid-twenties, remains involved almost forty years later. He explained that "What I know in volleyball, I want to teach kids" (June 2007). Likewise, Steve and Eli mentioned wanting to coach young people and help them hone their skills, while Kyle made a point of creating a nurturing environment for developing players in order to boost their confidence. One player was particularly invested in a specific group of young players because they were his friends' children. He returned to their team so that he could help them develop and ultimately play with them on the court.

Nick, long retired from playing, was especially interested in passing on nine-man volleyball, and thus remained involved with his old team in order to teach these techniques. One of these skills is the scissors style of setting the ball: unlike the Olympic style volley where the hands are above the forehead, in the scissors style of setting, the hands are at chest height and, upon receiving the ball, twist like the blades of a pair of scissors. Because the ball is set from chest height and is therefore hidden from view for a brief moment, an opponent has difficulty guessing the trajectory of the ball. In contrast, the ball remains visible when volleying from the forehead, allowing opposing teams to anticipate the next play. Nick also encouraged Michael to return and coach younger players so that traditional skills like the scissors style volley would be passed on, stating, "There's not that many like [Michael] who are in a position to pass it on. [...] If he retires, he takes along with him a lot of knowledge."

In addition, players feel that it is important to teach young and new players about the tournament's history. This is reiterated in "A Short History" as follows: each generation of players "[passes] down not only their skills and culture, but also continue[s] that part of the community's history. More than mere history, it is continuity and the building of ties between the generations" ("A short history" 1999, 26). Sharing stories can help to shape the experience and create a sense of connection among the participants. For example, the following anecdotes, related to the background of two historic teams, the New York Vikings and the Toronto Flying Tigers, were often shared with me and among the players. An interviewee explained that the Vikings had a Chinese name, Wing Fung, which is not a translation of Vikings but refers to the peak of a mountain. This name was given to the team because the strongest team at the time was Blue Eagle, "but we wanted to be higher than the eagle, because at the peak, at the Wing Fung, no eagle would go that high, where the clouds hang out and the peak is above the clouds." Another interviewee recounted how the Flying Tigers' logo was first designed with the wings closed, going down. This had to be changed because a senior member of the team indicated that "if the wings don't go up, we're never gonna win. And it's funny because it's a little bit of a Chinese superstition." Both participants shared these stories with enthusiasm and joy, one of them even recalling how the current Vikings players were always surprised and very happy to learn about how the team came to be known as Wing Fung. The story of the wings of the Flying Tigers has also become a part of the NACIVT history, as I found when other interviewees told me the story on separate occasions. Participants' interest in passing on this knowledge to new team members, and then later sharing it with me, shows that they enjoy recounting these histories, and that doing so fosters a bond between players, even between those early Vikings players who gave themselves the name Wing Fung and new players who were unaware of the Vikings' history.

The emphasis on passing down tournament history more broadly is also illustrated by the theme of the 63rd San Francisco tournament, "Embrace the Heritage," and the inclusion of a Classics Game where "Nine-man Legends" or alumni players were invited to play prior to the women's and men's final championship games. The goal was "to introduce the next generation of nine-man players [to ...] some of the game's history and honor those past great nine-man players" (*Classics game* 2007). One of the organizers reiterated the importance of educating players about the history of nine-man and described how this goal was integrated into the website by "collecting stories and blogs from participants or [inviting] past participants to talk about their experiences." Such initiatives are not new. In "A Short History" there are references to *lo chai* teams or "old wood teams," composed of players from the original teams that first started the tournament. Other teams could be admitted but had to "take on the name of one of the original teams. In this way, the original players and teams will be honored" (55th Tournament booklet 1999, 26).

Honouring the older generation of players and organizers served to confer respect, as well as remind the younger generation of the importance of these relationships and histories. Young players who showed their respect for elders were commended (Nick). Some players took this very seriously, seeking the blessing of elders if they planned to leave the team for a new club (Carl). Respect for elders was demonstrated in other ways, such as in forms of address and in bestowing awards. For example, two participants referred to older players in the circuit as "uncles." Though there may not be a blood relation, it is a "respectful term. Anybody that's older, […] you call them uncle as a sign of respect" (Nick). This sense of respect for older people is also reflected in the giving of awards at the banquet during the Labour Day tournaments. Honours were often bestowed on people and clubs that had made a significant contribution or commitment to the tournament as a way to "respect people who have been around, [and] give them face" (Steve). In addition, individuals who had passed away were eulogized in the tournament booklet (e.g., 58th Tournament booklet 2002; 61st Tournament booklet 2005), or in one instance, by having a local tournament organized in honour of a participant who had passed.

There is also recognition of the need to transfer positions of leadership to younger players (Nick, Kyle, Bill). One assistant coach pointed out, for example, that older teams need to help the younger teams so that they can ultimately take over. However, this is not always easy, since the "hardest thing is transitioning from older group to younger group; to get young people to take the role of the leaders" (Ira, September 2007). Recruiting and developing young players and ensuring new generations of players for a team are important not just among individual interviewees but for the viability of clubs as well. One US team that had won several championships is now defunct because "they got too old and they never drew young blood into the team" (Ken).

A number of players did express a keen desire to take up leadership positions as older players retire or step aside to give others a chance. At one of the oldest clubs in Toronto, veteran players seeking greater responsibility voluntarily formed committees to carry out various important tasks such as fundraising, taking attendance, and so on. Interviewees also gave examples of taking on more administrative roles in their clubs (August 2015). One interviewee became responsible for organizing the local tournaments when the people who usually organized the tournament wanted to retire. Kyle also shared that, when several of his teammates left the club, he became the team captain. He was groomed into this leadership position through frequent meetings with the coach and through receiving suggestions regarding issues that might arise. Similar mentoring has occurred for individuals learning to play in a new position (Mark).

In mentoring younger players and nurturing leadership skills, the clubs fostered qualities in the players that went beyond the volleyball court. For example, Peter explained that while his club was focused on moulding young athletes into good volleyball players, the club also helped them with issues relating to school and family problems. He viewed his club as having a community-service role, giving young people "something else besides maybe taking the wrong path, jail, doing drugs, whatever." Similarly, Diane indicated that the long-term plans of her club were to incorporate social programs to help young people, to get them off the street, improve their grades, and so on. Bill (23 years old, second generation) explained that his club went beyond teaching volleyball and wished to make good citizens off the court as well. While the club did not have specific programs, such as homework clubs or charity work, he felt that that the club provided a positive environment in various small ways, facilitating achievement outside of volleyball and resulting in something he called "the butterfly effect" (August 2015).

The emphasis on passing on traditions from one generation to the next served to highlight the importance of "generation" as a key construct through which the study participants interpreted their participation. They understood their participation in relation to earlier generations of immigrants who had struggled to survive in a new land, and to those players who first started playing nine-man and organized the tournament in the face of discrimination and other challenges. Generation also served as a signpost for their own involvement, where they identified themselves as part of the older or younger generation and referred to the obligations and desires that came with this position. There was a desire for continuity from one generation to the next, generally in terms of passing on the tradition of playing in the NACIVT and, more particularly, teaching specific NACIVT knowledge and history.

This understanding of generation and the passing on of traditions was gendered. For example, most male players recalled a male relative who was involved in and introduced them to the tournament. One exception was a woman whose father had played in the tournament and even founded one of the oldest teams in the circuit. She recalled that volleyball was part of her childhood and that she would practise volleying with her father inside the house so much that there were marks on the ceiling from the ball. By the time I interviewed her, she was no longer a competitive player, but she was still involved as a coach and hoped to continue her father's legacy. When I asked her what she expects of herself in relation to her volleyball club, she responded that, "My dad has started [the club] and the way we saw the club and envisioned it … I continued to pursue that." While this former player's commitment is commendable, it was rare to hear women's participation celebrated in the same way. Indeed, it was often presumed that women would not continue participating after marriage or having children. Thus, continuity of involvement, exemplified in the unbroken line of players from one generation to the next, was seen as patrilineal, from grandfather to father to sons, with little mention of continuity from grandmothers to mothers to daughters.

Moreover, belief in the importance of teaching volleyball knowledge to younger players was specific to the nine-man game. The skills and techniques that are unique to nine-man volleyball were specifically identified as needing to be preserved and passed down. This special knowledge remains within the domain of men, therefore, since women play sixes (see chapter 3). Similarly, the importance of teaching the younger players about the history of the NACIVT also centres on nine-man, with little celebration of or even teaching about the women's game and its history. With the exception of the local tournament that was organized in memory of a former player, most elders who were remembered and honoured were men, further highlighting how the continuity of generation is patrilineal. The lack of women in leadership positions or even considered as elders (chapter 3) can impact whether younger female players are groomed into positions of leadership in the same way that the men are. Since this mentoring happens within teams and is done by those who are already in positions of power, those clubs that have both women's and men's teams would have to engage in this preparation and training consciously and be sensitive to the lack of women in leadership roles.

It is likely that in the specific context of the NACIVT, the emphasis on generational continuity, respect for elders, and conformity was reinforced by the values and culture of sports more generally. For example, because of the team-sport environment, the interviewees' experiences were often shaped by dynamics relating to the hierarchy of players. John (November 2006), for example, referred to the importance for rookies of listening to their coaches and to veteran players. He also explained that rookies were expected to ease the burden on veteran players by bringing them water or food (a point also mentioned by Irene). Back talk was not tolerated; should rookies step out of line, he noted, such individuals and their behaviour would be disciplined through embarrassing, harsh, or even degrading initiation rituals. Perhaps because John was no longer a rookie, he was not critical of these hierarchies and seemed to support punishment of rookies through hazing rituals. On the other hand, one former player recalled being berated by the coach during the middle of match. The respondent described how the coach was "*screaming* at me, like we're in the middle of the competition, and he'd run up and he'd be yelling at me and just screaming."

Such verbal abuse was not uncommon (Ava: 35 years old, second generation; Helen). For example, Nancy, who joined a team as an adolescent, recalled feeling intimidated by an older player in her late teens. The older teammate was very vocal with her frustration when players did not perform well, usually younger players whose skills had not yet developed. Nancy felt scared and even cried as a result of this particular player. This fear was reiterated by Amber when I asked her to tell me her impressions of her first tryout:

> The older ladies were very competitive, and whenever I made a mistake, they were kinda … not so much yell, but strongly encouraged to do certain things, kinda help you along, but in a not so nice way. So that kinda … I didn't like that. It kinda scared me from returning. (July 2005)

Similarly, Lisa explained that "when you're younger as well, you tend to get intimidated by older people, especially older people that you look up to, not only in terms of life but for volleyball, I mean" (May 2007). Lisa ultimately switched to a team that had players who were close to her in age and facing similar issues (e.g., graduating from high school, choosing post-secondary education, etc.). Interestingly, when I interviewed Phoebe, she too mentioned feeling intimidated by the older players at her first tryout, not just because of age but because some of the players were well known in club and elite volleyball circles.

For two interviewees, the age gap and hierarchy were obstacles for their continued participation. Both players found that the teams they first joined were not welcoming to younger players. The leaders on the two teams were uninterested in player development. As a result, these interviewees felt discouraged, and one player quit altogether and did not return to nine-man volleyball for a few years. When he rejoined, he wanted to

> prove to them that I … that I … that I could be a good player and you shouldn't treat … because everybody starts off at being not good, probably. You can call it whatever you want, but when you're

learning something new, even in school or whatever, you're not good at it. So you know just to prove to them that you shouldn't be treated this way.

Ultimately, he still found that the focus was on the older players and that there was a lack of interest in developing younger players. He therefore left the team and formed another club. The other participant, after consulting with his father (another example of the generational influence), honoured his commitment to the team for the first season but later changed teams.

Another player shared how this hierarchical relationship was instilled in other ways throughout the course of the season. She stated that "A lot of the coaching staff and a lot of the veterans on the teams kept telling us rookies that you have to pay your dues, you can't always expect to start, if you come to practice early, help set up, work really hard at practices, you'll be rewarded for that." During fundraising activities, she also recalled being reminded that younger players should be grateful to older players, who did not necessarily need to fundraise for the club, since they were employed and would be able to pay for team- and tournament-related expenses without fundraising. As a young player, she was "reminded after practices that the older players are doing it for the future of the younger players."

Other teams did not adhere so strictly to player hierarchies but did have a ranking of players based on skills, such that the "A-Team," for example, would be the best players, followed by the "B" and "C" teams, whose members might require more training. On one team, for example, there was less of an expectation that the B and C team players would set up and take down the nets; rather the A players modelled the expected behaviour of responsibility and cooperation (Toronto Unit team practice, August 2015). As one alumni player from the team put it, "We don't eat our young." In other words, this team does not treat incoming recruits poorly or make them do menial tasks simply because they are rookies. Instead, as I noticed at the practice, senior players modelled the expected behaviour, showing collaboration and cooperation with one another.

The sports environment and its emphasis on loyalty and respect for team hierarchies could, on the other hand, foster supportive, nurturing, and mentoring relations. For example, many alumni players remain involved with their teams or clubs. Kyle described how a retired player travelled to the New York Mini "to watch us because with our players, a lot of them do support us still, just because it's the tradition of our team" (March 2007). In one Toronto club, former players volunteer to help out at tournaments – for example, by providing massages and water; one alumnus even flew from across the country to assist. Another club that was established almost thirty years ago had a more structured relationship, running an annual social event with a fundraising component at which old and new players gathered in order to support the younger players.

Some players shared personal anecdotes about when they felt supported by senior players. Sarah (May 2015) noted how her coaches helped her through difficult times, such as during the breakup of a relationship. Steve also shared the following anecdote when asked about a memorable experience at his first tournament:

> I was serving the ball and one of the older, one of my older teammates [Fred] came up to me and he said "Hey, listen, I know you're the youngest guy on the team, but I just want you to know you have the best serve on our team." And that really stuck to my mind 'cause he made me feel so important, he made me feel so good and he made me feel like it doesn't matter how young you are, you're accepted on our team. So those words I'll never forget. And that particular moment, I'll never forget.

Similarly, Mark fondly recalled how older teammates "were really trying to make an effort to make me feel comfortable and a lot of guys were kinda taking me under their wing and stuff, so it's very, it was a very nurturing type of environment" (March 2007).

Beyond volleyball, Eli also appreciated how

> we really take care of each other ... if someone needs advice on something, we feel comfortable talking to the older guys about it, and

the older guys are totally comfortable, you know, taking them aside or whatever and showing them the ropes or, you know, even through email and stuff like that. If you need any help with anything, not just volleyball, they're very willing to help without any sort of judging.

It is clear that a number of players felt supported, inspired, and mentored by older teammates. While there is risk of reinforcing an "old boys network," those clubs that did have both men's and women's teams made an effort to socialize together and help one another.

In addition to being a source of encouragement, older players served as role models and inspiration for younger, incoming players, a function that is particularly important in the realm of sports where historically there are few well-known and successful Asian athletes. Nick recalled an older player whom he particularly admired, someone who was nicknamed "The Hammer" because he could hit the ball with such power. Likewise, when I asked Amber to describe her impressions of participating in her first tournament, she said,

> I was just [...] in awe of the older women actually and how good they were at volleyball. It was a really good experience just seeing that level of volleyball and aspiring to be like them. I was playing middle at the time and [Paula] was actually playing on [another] team ... and she's like five foot three and playing middle, and middles, usually, you have to be the tallest person to play. And I was just amazed at her skill and I was, like, "I just want to be like her!"

Other players reiterated these feelings of admiration and inspiration (e.g., Christie, Brian, Lisa). Christie felt that seeing strong, highly skilled, competitive women from various cities, some of whom were not particularly tall, inspired her to strive to be an equally skilled player. Having Asian athletes as role models was especially important, as the interviewees had noted the lack of Asian volleyball players in the mainstream leagues in which they had competed, and was especially critical for countering the dominant stereotypes about Asian masculinity (i.e., unathletic) and

Asian femininity (i.e., submissive, and passive). Given the lack of status of women's volleyball within the NACIVT and beyond, it is worth noting that young Asian women still found inspiring role models within the NACIVT.

Occasionally, the sporting context resulted in conflicts with the values of generational continuity and deference to one's elders. For example, Steve was one of the younger players on his team when he first began participating. He felt quite nervous at his first tournament, "wanting to perform for the older teammates," and was also conscious of playing against adults. Later, even after he had played for many years, age differences were still a salient factor in his experience. As Steve's skills improved, he was asked to take on a leadership and then a coaching role. He found this especially challenging because "sometimes you have to point a finger and order [...] and I certainly didn't like to tell my elders what to do." This was echoed by Rob when he explained how he had to negotiate age differences when playing with individuals who were older and more experienced:

> One thing in Chinese tradition, right, [is] to be respectful of your elders, ancient tradition. So I was very conscious of that. I would not overtly criticize [one particular older player] in anything. If anything I would offer a suggestion on this or that. But I had to hold it all in, right? [...] And when older players were not leading by example, it became very difficult again. So that was quite frustrating, and in those situations, the age factor did come into play, because if that older player had been younger, I probably would have used a different tactic to deal with it. But because he was an older player, I had to kind of – I spoke my mind, I told him what I thought, but I had to still be somewhat measured.

Thus, for both Steve and Rob, being named as leaders on their respective teams because of skill and ability, and subsequently needing to give direction to older players, proved challenging because of the consciousness of generational differences and the expectation of showing deference to elders.

In another example, generational, age, and team seniority hierarchies conflicted with tournament work assignments when younger players were responsible for being court monitors in a match between teams of older players. At the Captain's Meeting (1 September 2006) for the Washington Tournament, one of the organizers asked players not to pick on younger court monitors. Those in attendance laughed in response, but this issue could be a potentially serious challenge. For example, when I asked Owen what happened if players had problems with the referees, he recalled the impact of monitors who were young and inexperienced when he was playing against another top-level team during a critical match:

> We had these thirteen- and fourteen-year-old kids in our pool and they ended up reffing that game. They didn't know what they were doing (laughs). And some of our players, they were just screaming at the poor kids. I thought they were going to cry (laughs). I felt so bad, but what are you going to do, right?

The emphasis on winning could result in conflict, especially if teams felt that referees were not officiating properly. In this example, it is evident that the unique sporting context of the NACIVT and the shifting roles that younger and older players have to take up in running the tournament can challenge the expectation to defer to veteran players or one's elders.

Likewise, the view that tradition should be cherished unquestionably may not be shared by all, especially by those whose primary goal is playing and winning rather than upholding long standing customs. For example, Nancy stated that the opening ceremonies usually include a lion dance and, while "everybody likes seeing the lion dance because it's tradition," she admitted that "you wanna get [the ceremonies] over quick though, that's the thing too, you really do wanna get it over quick." Adam also recalled that, as a coach, he emphasized the importance of tradition, such as the practice of waking up early to participate in the pre-tournament parade through Chinatown:

> That was something that was difficult for people to understand, that this is part of the tournament. You don't just go there to play, you don't just show up at 9:05 waiting for your game at 9:15. You have to be part

of the tradition, and the tradition says that you march, you do the little parade with the rest of the team, you hold a banner saying who you are and you follow the lion dance and so forth. So that was difficult for [players] to understand.

This sense of lack of interest in traditional elements like the lion dance, the opening ceremonies, or the parade was salient during the two Labour Day tournaments that I observed. During the Toronto tournament, for example, participation was sparse in the parade to the tournament site, which was led by a lion dance, and throughout the opening ceremonies I observed numerous volleyballs in the air, as players practised and warmed up rather than paying attention to the opening speeches. These examples serve as a reminder of the ever-present gaps or fissures within community (Edwards 2001), including generational differences.

Generation Gap

"Generation gap" is a common phrase used to describe conflict-ridden relationships within immigrant communities. It is usually assumed that "generation" refers to parents (or the first generation of immigrants), and that the second generation is native-born/raised children. Tensions arise, it is assumed, from the different degrees of assimilation that occur or do not occur between the generations. This approach has been criticized for reproducing the vertical analysis common in Asian American studies (Lowe 1996), and for importing the weaknesses of the assimilation framework. Nevertheless, "generation" remained a meaningful construct for the participants, particularly the differences between the generations. Even with an expressed commitment to honouring those who came before them and to respecting their elders, the interviewees experienced and negotiated "generation gaps," particularly as they grew older.

Age gaps, for instance, heightened differences in priorities, values, and common interests. Irene (April 2007), for example, remarked that while unity among players was heavily promoted, there were a few players on her team who already had children, and these players tended to socialize together on their own. In fact, there was very little interaction between the oldest and youngest players in her club. Steve explained that it was difficult to be close with everyone on his team because of the large age gap. One coach was mindful of this difference between himself and the players, and while there is a sense of regret over this inability to connect totally with the players, he interprets this as a show of respect:

> The kids playing now, they're in their teens, twenties, they look at you and there's always a bit of a line drawn. [...] I'm not in tune with what's going on and they, I don't think they feel totally at ease and be themselves when I'm coaching. I guess it's [inaudible] that bit of sense of respect, "Oh he's an old geezer coming here, watch what we say to this guy" (laughs).

From the other side of the spectrum, Kyle found that he did not socialize as much with the older players who had children, while at the same time he felt that the younger players were too young for him with their non-stop carousing on weekends. Nancy also found herself increasingly feeling disconnected from the younger players' "more wild" ways, which she attributed to their age. Ultimately, she no longer felt comfortable being a member of the team and explained it as a "need to be with people that kind of think the same."

Age differences also manifested themselves in varying financial responsibilities. For example, Karen stated that participation in team dinners was strongly encouraged by coaches and older players as an opportunity for teams and players to bond. However, many young players had part-time jobs and did not always have the disposable income to participate consistently. She recalled that once in a while an older person would help pay, but "we would hear murmurs about well, you know, you don't have a mortgage to pay, you don't have children to feed."

While being an older player may afford some benefits such as greater status or greater freedom, there is an additional sense of responsibility that comes with being a senior member of the team.

Christie recalled the challenge of teaching new players and being a positive example to the new recruits. She even likened the experience to babysitting. Sarah admitted that she too felt as though she was a "babysitter" for the younger players on her team, and that she was valued only for this role, rather than as a volleyball player (May 2015). In some cases, older players felt it necessary to reprimand younger players for inappropriate behaviour, such as underage drinking, particularly since they felt that the parents of these players were entrusting them with their children. This sense of responsibility was less gendered by comparison with my witnessing of middle-aged women who took on the caregiver and food provider roles at the tournament. Senior male players were just as likely to feel a sense of responsibility for the younger players' behaviour, reflecting perhaps the influence of the sporting context in shaping gender norms.

Supervising and managing younger players may be less of a challenge or may have changed during the last decade, however, as one player observed that helicopter parenting has become increasingly the norm. She said that, by contrast with when she was a young, rookie player, it is now common for parents to drive children to and from and even attend practices or tournaments, even the Labour Day tournament (Sarah, May 2015). The head of the Toronto Unit team also noted that he speaks with parents of new players when they attend the first practice to "reassure them, talk to them" that their children are in good hands, after which, the parents do not attend subsequent sessions. Parents' attendance at practices or tryouts was not common in mid-2000 when I first began this study. When I asked about this new responsibility, he sighed in a way that seemed to suggest that this could be onerous. Nevertheless, he joked that one parent was so committed to the team that she deserved a team t-shirt (August 2015). The increased parental presence at practices and the tournaments signals a clear difference from when I first began studying the NACIVT, when players recounted bonding with other players during the long public-transit commute home from practices, and recalled the thrill of travelling with the team without parental supervision.

There were also generational differences that went beyond language, priorities, and common interests, and were sources of tension or disagreement. For example, Nick described conflicts with a former coach when he was a player. He explained that the coach was

> from the older generation, he runs things very autocratically. Do it my way or the highway, and no one would dare speak back to him, [...] when you get somebody like that, the fact that he was older in age [...] I mean you wouldn't dare [question him].

The son of a founding member of a club with a forty-year history also described the differences between him and his father in much the same way. Another player also found that there were conflicts on his former team where "the people coming in are different than the traditional, old school, regimented people that are there now, that are running the place."

Generational differences and gender were sometimes cited as the reason for the lack of change within the tournament. For example, Adam shared how he encountered resistance from "the old people" when new forms of advertising were introduced to the tournament, involving placards lining the side of the court. In particular, when discussing the eligibility rule, players (e.g., Peter, Karen, Amber, and Christie) placed the blame on "the old men" (Amber) and their continued influence on the organization of the tournament (see also chapter 3). The lack of attention paid to the women's game was also an issue that was linked to the "older generation" (Lisa).

Where younger players positioned themselves as more open to new ideas than the older generation, Nick seemed to think otherwise, lamenting how younger players dismissed his advice with respect to certain skills that are unique to nine-man volleyball. Another player felt that it was too late to try and teach these skills to younger players. Despite the celebration of passing on traditions and knowledge from one generation to the next, in reality, efforts to teach and share these skills were not always welcomed. One technique that was not being passed on involved palming and throwing the ball. Nick explained that the original method was very subtle, and the holding of the ball was barely detectable. However, the new, younger players are not able to master the intricacy of the skill and "it's like a basketball dunk. It's like Vince Carter jumping up there and grabbing the ball and they really really hold it and throw it down." His observation seems to suggest that the younger players are influenced by mainstream sports like basketball and have imported basketball techniques into the nine-man game.

Nick was making an effort to pass on these skills, but was having difficulty. He speculated that some young players accepted it, while "others say, 'Okay, old guy' (laughs)" and dismiss him or "They think you're crazy … I've been trying to teach it to our guys, but every day it's an argument." This disappointment was also expressed at tournaments, as older former players are often heard "talking in Toisanese, criticizing technique" from the sidelines (Diane).

Bridging Generation Gaps

Despite the frustration expressed by some younger players over the resistance to change of the older generation and by older players over the lack of respect for traditional skills, some players who now had children playing in the circuit as well as some alumni in their late fifties saw the tournament as a vehicle for bringing people of different generations together by providing "a common ground of communication," a way to build ties between the generations ("A short history" 1999, 26). One player in his late fifties, for example, joyfully described how, the night before the tournament, he was sitting with some players in their mid-twenties and others who were high school students, and they were all enjoying themselves. Ken (September 2007) reiterated this connection, saying that the tournament was an opportunity for "different generations getting together, sitting with [people in their] twenties, thirties, high school kids. We embraced them, now the younger kids embrace the next generation." There are also teams that include players ranging in age from their early teens to their late fifties and early sixties. Nevertheless, while this may be a point of celebration, when I asked Lisa to comment, she astutely observed that "it's great that [let's say a] twelve-year-old kid is playing with that thirty-year-old man. Like that's awesome, but me being that twelve-year-old, I'd think wow, thirty, he's more than half [meaning double] my age. It's a different perspective I think." On the other hand, Nick recalled the thrill of hanging out with older players when he first began participating as a young teenager.

In light of the sense of intimidation that many players recounted when they first joined a team, the view that the tournament brings together different generations may be only superficially accurate. For example, several players mentioned and appreciated the presence of older Chinese fans who came to watch the tournament:

> There's always the crowd of old Chinese guys that come in from, it doesn't matter what city, there's always some guys that are like "Oh, yeah, back in the day, back in the thirties or back in the fifties" ... there's always some really old guys and they're always yelling in Chinese at people and that was the first time that I ... that I saw the old Chinese guys and every year there's always that group. That was good. (Mark; June 2007)

The presence of these older fans was vividly captured in Liang's (2014) documentary on the NACIVT. Although their presence left an impression on Mark at his first tournament, his recollection of older fans is limited to an observation and he does not mention any interaction or conversation with them, calling into question how effectively the tournament serves to connect people across generations. Conversely, Lisa indicated that, through talking with players who were close in age to her parents, she came to understand better the struggles that her parents' generation had experienced, their yearning for civil and religious freedom and economic opportunities, and "about duty and obligation and how important the two concepts are within the Chinese culture. Definitely made me understand why I make some of the decisions I do." This example illustrates how "generation" remains a salient entry point in understanding relationships within Chinese and Asian communities (see also Chin 2016).

The importance of these vertical relationships and their role in creating continuity were reiterated by Michael, someone who has been involved in the tournament for many years and was active in the Chinese American community. When I asked him what made the NACIVT significant for the Chinese American community, he insisted that the tournament provided a vehicle for participants to

> come to our community, either in volleyball or some sort of involvement in the community, do something in the community and learn about the roots, about helping the community. [...] In a way that's good for them too, to let them know that hey there's a background, it's a great one, it's a great tradition. It brings the community together, and it gives a chance for the youth of the Chinese or the Asian background a chance to meet and to share the Asian culture. So I think that is the big aspect of the tournament, and that's what we try to pass on to generations, year to year, that tradition.

Thus, the vertical relationships between generations that the tournament nurtures, such as connecting with one's roots, could potentially facilitate lateral, horizontal connections through meeting other Chinese or Asian youth.

The generation gap could manifest as a language barrier, especially in the early years of the tournament when first-generation players who spoke little English encountered locally born and English-speaking young people. While the latter were interested in participating, they were not able to communicate with the then-active players. One interviewee recalled that his team was able to connect with players who were born in the United States and could not speak the language of the older teams and players:

> I could communicate with the young players and there was no young people before [my team] ... so there was a big influx of people that are willing and want to learn the game. [...] I mean, our [team] happened to be there to do the transition for them. Because before that, [the

older players and the younger players] don't communicate! [The older players] don't speak English, or they have no, they cannot relate to the young kids that are there.

This type of linguistic bridge building is referenced by other players (e.g., Peter, Rob). For example, Peter described how the generation gap could be bridged by his ability to speak different Chinese dialects: the younger players "couldn't order food in the Chinese restaurant, they couldn't communicate, so uh ... and sometimes when the sponsors were speaking or they had delegates speaking, they wouldn't know what they were talking about, so we would translate for them" (May 2007). A retired player also found that he too had to play the role of a "cultural linguistic bridge [between players] from China and the Canadian-born Chinese." He later suggested that this successful integration of players was a significant factor in his team's success. This is a variation of the mediating between groups noted by Ng (1996), who found that second-generation Chinese people in Vancouver saw themselves as cultural and linguistic interpreters who bridged the gap between the Chinese minority and mainstream society in Canada.

The vertical relationships discussed above are gendered, in part because of the structure of the tournament and of volleyball. Hierarchical relationships among players, for example, were inevitably along gendered lines because teams were separated by gender. Nine-man and the tournament were frequently introduced into the lives of young men through gendered connections – through fathers, older brothers, and/or cousins. The elders were usually male, and thus examples of acknowledging honorific relationships were also frequently gendered, with few examples, both given and observed, of mothers, grandmothers, "aunts," and sisters being honoured and respected, serving as coaches, or being consulted for guidance. In contrast, horizontal and lateral relationships seemed to sometimes cut across lines of gender, race, and class. These connections were based on the invention of new traditions.

New Traditions and Connections

It was clear that Luke was feeling nervous about being back at a nine-man tournament. He took his time after parking the car to gather his gear, checking again if he had forgotten anything, and whether he had locked the car door. Luke was a competitive person who loved sports, especially volleyball, and so the nerves were in part due to the upcoming day of play, for which he had not trained. But Luke had also stopped playing in part because of conflicts with his former coach. Nevertheless, Luke had friends who still played, and they were eager to have him join a team that they had pulled together at the last minute to play in the tournament. Luke arrived early; the rest of the players from his team were not yet there, and he stood in the middle of the parking lot, scanning the scene for a familiar face. He looked lost, for unlike others, he did not have a group with whom to congregate, set up, or warm up. Then, from across the lot, someone shouted his name, and a group of young men and women rushed over to greet him. They were clearly delighted to see Luke as they exchanged warm hugs and greetings. They were not the individuals he was going to play with throughout the day, but they were nonetheless happy to see him, and Luke consequently looked more at ease.

Over the course of the day, I saw Luke giving and receiving high fives, hugs, and encouragement and greeting and chatting with friends new and old. It was undeniable that Luke was reconnecting with the nine-man community. It was this community that supported players who had gone through difficult times like losing a parent, a relationship breakup, or moving cities. I was reminded of other tournaments I had attended where I would witness many happy reunions between individuals who had not seen each other since the previous year, the joy in competing and winning together, and the camaraderie that players forged. It is these relationships and friendships that are deeply meaningful for the NACIVT participants. While narrow categories of Asianness and Chineseness may frame their involvement, the lived experience of competing in the NACIVT and the relationships that are cultivated within the

NACIVT community – *their* community – are what bring players back year after year.

That the NACIVT players form a community is perhaps best reflected in interviewees' loyalty to the tournament and the desire of many players to "give back" through coaching or volunteering to help organize the tournament. Moreover, interviewees articulated notions of belonging, comfort, and a family-like environment – all terms associated with community – in their description of what was most significant about their participation in the NACIVT, irrespective of whether they were situated in Canada or the United States. Indeed, no differences were observed between US and Canadian participants with respect to the types and meaning of relationships forged. Nevertheless, following Brah (1996) and Clifford (1997), the notion of community is not used as an explanation for understanding the NACIVT but as a point of departure.

In their writing on diaspora, Brah (1996) and Clifford (1997) are critical of the focus in the scholarship on "elsewhere" or "homeland," a focus that can neglect those who choose not to or cannot move (see also Ang 2001; Anthias 1998). Instead, both Lowe (1996) and Clifford (1997) advocate a horizontal and lateral approach, respectively, to understand relationships between people. Clifford (1997), for example, urges scholars to question the assumption that diaspora's centre is the point of origin and proposes that "decentered, lateral connections ... and a shared ongoing history of displacement, suffering, adaptation or resistance may be as important as the projection of a specific origin" (250). In other words, in examining the production of diaspora, rather than paying exclusive attention to how members relate to a presumed common origin or shared identity, Clifford would have us focus on how people connect with others despite or across difference.

Lateral relations refer to those relationships and flows that are not connected through and with a centre or point of origin (Clifford, 1997. Like Clifford, Lowe (1996) questions the presumed direction of the transfer of culture and knowledge, but where Clifford focuses his critique on "homeland" or "point of origin," Lowe is specifically referring to the vertical passing of knowledge from one generation to the next. She calls for contextualizing horizontal within vertical relations in order to expand the analytic lens beyond familial and hierarchical relationships. When we take lateral and horizontal relations into account, partially overlapping networks that connect several communities of people come into view. This could be interpreted in different ways, such as Brah's (1996) contention of thinking about intersecting diasporas or Voigt-Graf's (2004) work on different diasporic nodes, shifting cultural hearths, and new centres of diaspora. In displacing the central role of the "point of origin," a focus on lateral and horizontal relations represents a more dynamic and fluid approach to diaspora, and makes space for unexpected relationships and links. Furthermore, with such a focus, new and meaningful traditions and practices that bond people across and through difference come into view.

Perhaps, the most salient factor that brings the players together is their passion for volleyball and for being members of the same volleyball community, be it the same team, the same club, or the circuit as a whole. As Patrick (May 2015) and others (Ava, May 2015) put it, "that love for volleyball ... that's why we're all going," a love so great that "you wanna play on concrete you know" (Sarah, May 2015). Indeed, without an avid interest in the sport among people in Washington, Boston, Montreal, and so on, the main Labour Day tournament and the smaller local tournaments like the New York Mini would not exist. Volleyball is an important pastime for many of the participants: James (March 2007) observed that he encountered the same players in NACIVT, mainstream regular sixes, and beach volleyball tournaments. The importance and enjoyment of playing volleyball cannot be dismissed, as is reflected in Diane's response when I asked her to tell me about her most memorable tournament:

We had a summer where we would never forget [said slowly, nostalgically]. We got together, practised every single weekend. [...] Practices were set for certain days of the week, but say if on a Wednesday I felt like playing, I would call a few people and say "Do you wanna play volleyball today?" and *everybody* would come out for practice. [...] People like playing enough that, even if it's not a set practice day, we can get people together.

Diane's recollection demonstrates that she and her teammates were linked by a common love of volleyball, commitment to the team, and a desire to play. While they might have learned volleyball from a coach or from an older family member, the connection was not a shared knowledge of Chinese culture or Asianness that is passed down from generation to generation, but the shared experience of playing and enjoying this sport.

Similarly, when asked to recall her most memorable tournament, Carol described her close relationships with her teammates. Again, being of Asian descent was not the key factor in facilitating intimate bonds. Rather, Carol explained that they connected because "we all lived in close quarters and spent every minute of that [tournament] weekend together. We also played very well together and bonded on the court" (June 2007). Ava (35 years old, second generation) also described how one tournament was particularly memorable because her team had struggled to feel united, as a result of conflicts arising between the players. Ultimately, she said "we did pull together at the end," and the team was far more successful in the tournament than anticipated. Ava was particularly moved by the fact that they had come together because of a love for volleyball and that the experience "was really fulfilling." Likewise, Luke valued his relationships with his teammates a great deal, making sure that they were staying positive and focused, and that they were enjoying themselves. Indeed, spending time with his teammates with whom he had practised and worked so hard leading up to the tournament was what he looked forward to the most in the days leading up to Labour Day. As he put it, "that sort of camaraderie and fellowship is an amazing feeling."

Even in situations where Asianness or Chineseness could have been drawn on to explain relationships, volleyball was the significant factor. For example, Lisa described how difficult it was for her to explain to her coach and teammates that she had decided to change teams, taking considerable time to determine how best to approach them and to share the news:

You don't want to burn any bridges because the community is so small, and you do end up often times practising with each other, scrimmaging with each other, and you *definitely* do see each other at the tournaments as well. So it was difficult.

For Lisa, the community that could be disrupted as a result of her decision was not a Chinese or Asian community but her volleyball community. The difficulty she experienced was a result of the knowledge that she needed to maintain good relationships with her teammates because teams often practised, scrimmaged, and played with each other. Whereas a vertical analysis might assume that Lisa and her teammates shared common values that were passed down to them from their Chinese parents and that it was *these* beliefs that provided a compass for her in trying to navigate this dilemma, Lisa's own words showed that she was more concerned with maintaining good relationships with her fellow volleyball players in order to facilitate practising and playing with them in the future.

Knowing that NACIVT participants shared a common interest in volleyball fostered new friendships. Mark, for example, said that it was fairly easy to talk to people: "A lot of the time you can just kinda just walk up and be like 'How'd you guys do today?' or, you know, just start the small talk about the tournament." Interacting with strangers was simple because "everybody's got something in common [i.e., volleyball] so it's not hard to break the ice." Ira expressed a similar sense of familiarity by stating that "To me, even if you don't know everybody, you kind of know everybody, you might recognize them, seen them before or played against them." Likewise, Lisa recalled how she met people in the tournament, specifically through the shared experience of defeat. Her team had suffered a disappointing loss early in the tournament, preventing them from advancing to the finals. The team decided to

> drown our sorrows in alcohol, and it seemed like, it seemed like a lot of people were in that situation as well. So I remember just being in the hotel and … riding around in the trolley, the baggage trolley with people from San Francisco, L.A., just some friends that you kinda made along the way.

Irrespective of whether these relationships became deep and meaningful, it is relevant that Lisa felt that she was not alone in her disappointment and that she connected with other people. Volleyball facilitated these friendships.

Volleyball and participating in the NACIVT became a tradition that connected participants. Michael, for example, explained that "Part of the great thing that I enjoy is to know good people, that we share the same interests. You know we could relate to each other: 'San Francisco?' 'Yes!' already even without asking 'San Francisco for what?' (laughs)." Michael was recalling an incident where he ran into another player during the off season and, when they recognized each other, rather than saying hello, this person simply said "San Francisco?" and Michael knew that he was asking whether he would be attending the upcoming tournament there. These connections may be reinforced by subsequent participation in tournaments. For example, at the Captain's Meeting (1 September 2006), the speaker noted that, "those of us who've been to the last three New York Minis know rain delays happen" (Field Notes, Washington Tournament), and there was a murmur of agreement. This reference to previous participation and subsequent displays of personal experience are a demonstration of these connections to each other. In another case, one person noted in the Guest Book of the original NACIVT website how *"[W]e all know* the logistical nightmare(s) of running an outdoor tourney" (*NACIVT.com guest book* n.d., emphasis in original). Another implores, "I don't understand why it *always* rains on the last day?" (*NACIVT.com guest book* n.d., emphasis added). One can just imagine others nodding their heads in agreement. Such sharing of experiences reinforces the lateral connections between participants.

In theorizing horizontal connections, Lowe (1996) points out that culture is not transferred as a complete and unchanged entity from the "root" to elsewhere. She suggests that culture can be worked out horizontally in meaningful ways. The connections made between players through volleyball clearly illustrate this important point. Nine-man volleyball is no longer played in Toisan, the supposed homeland of this game and the root of this Chinese cultural form. However, it continues to thrive in diaspora and has come to signify a vital example of Chinese culture and form of identification. Indeed, a team from China participated in the 2014 Las Vegas tournament, and I was told that the team had never played nine-man before and was being taught how to play as they were competing! Thus, nine-man volleyball is a practice that has flourished to a great extent through horizontal links and not solely through a commitment to preserving unchanged cultural practices being passed down from one generation to the next.

Horizontal connections established through similar age or circumstances were also evident. Often participants' feelings of being able to relate to one another were *not* via "Chineseness," "Asianness," or an assumption of common ethnicity, heritage, or culture. Mark, for example, explained how he felt disconnected from his teammates who were five or six years older than he was, and so at his first tournament he spent more time with another team that had players closer to his own age and little time with his own teammates. Lisa experienced an age gap as well, but where Mark chose to continue to play with his team, Lisa decided to switch to another club. She shared how she came to the decision to play for another team with people her own age:

> I *really* enjoyed playing with people closer to my age, and there was just so many things that I could relate to more, being in high school and being on the cusp of going to university or going to college and having more things in common, having more fun at that age.

In Lisa's case, and that of other players such as Nancy, being close in age and facing similar circumstances such as school and decisions about the future were the key factors in helping her feel a sense of connection with her teammates rather than an assumed common "Chineseness."

Another horizontal connection fostered via presumed shared circumstances is the relationship between participants who identified themselves as "half-Asian" or "halfies" (Mark, Christie, Helen). As Helen jokingly put it, "you always notice mixed kids when you're mixed" (May 2015). While Mark said that he does not necessarily seek out others "like him" even if he notices them, he admitted that "we all kinda hang out." Similarly, Eli seemed to think that other "half" players gravitated towards each other because "we're a mixed culture I think, and I think we have that in common, and we have a little bit of the Chinese plus you know we feel like ... we're more ... Canadian ... or more ... we have other influences. [...] We relate better." While Eli asserted a sense of relating to one another, he clearly had difficulty articulating why. This may have been in part because "most single racial identities are given. For multiracial people, you live your racial narrative by creating it" (Spickard 2001, 93). Thus, the hesitation and difficulty that Eli experienced in trying to explain this sense of connection or Mark's vague description of this relationship may be because it is based on changing and dynamic identities, ones that are not necessarily grounded in already established categories. Furthermore, the ambivalence that "halfies" felt in answering questions around their identification with each other was likely because my question of whether they related to each other as fellow "half-Asian" people was still in a context that assumed racial identity as given and static. I asked this question based on the assumption that they did not fit into the category of "Asian" or "Chinese" and therefore would bond as a result. In doing so, I assumed that they would "develop solidarity simply by virtue of their mutual isolation" (de Finney 2010, 472) and ignored how they are multiply located and that the narrative of their sense of belonging is still in process.

While Mark was vague and Eli had difficulty explaining their sense of connection to other "halfies," Christie gave a detailed account of her sense of identification with a teammate who was also "half-Asian." I had enquired if she is often asked "What are you?," and she quickly agreed and began talking about "standing out" in her childhood because of her mixed racial background. She then proceeded to recall moments when she connected with others whom she saw as "half, like her." For example, she shared a conversation she had with an opponent during a high school soccer game: "I was like, 'Hey, are you half-Asian?' and she's like, 'Yeah,' and I'm like, 'Half what?' 'Chinese.' 'Me too! Who's Chinese?' 'My mom.' 'Me too! What's your name?' '[Sharon].' 'I'm [Christie], we both have White names!'" The sense of connection, while superficial, is clear in the excitement that Christie expresses when realizing how much she had in common with another player who was also "half-Asian" and that she was therefore not alone. Later, when Christie was trying out for an NACIVT volleyball team, she felt isolated because she did not know anyone else at the tryout or on the team, and "it was all full Chinese girls." Christie wondered if

> that other half girl's gonna show up from soccer. And I saw her open the door and looked around and she didn't know anyone, and then she saw me and she runs across the gym and she's like, "Hey, remember me?" and I'm like, "Yeah, I remember you."

The importance of this connection was reinforced by a childhood of feeling that she was different from others and alone in her difference: "When I was younger, I remember once being like twelve years old and there was some other girl who was like eight, and she was half-Asian, and I'm like, 'Oh, my god, there's *another one!*'" (emphasis added). Even her reference to "that *other* half girl" (emphasis added) suggests that Christie did not know many "half-Asian" girls.

Christie's experience suggests a profound sense of identification with those who were "half," one that was linked to experiences of feeling alone, isolated, and judged. Nevertheless, for other interviewees who (were) identified as "half" or mixed race, this sense of connection was tentative and inexplicable in some cases. The literature is more aligned with Christie's experience, such that "there appears to be a commonality, a level of comfort, a place where one does not have to code-switch, a level of unspoken understanding, that is experienced by mixed race in the company of others like them that is not found in their experiences with monoracial people" (Mengel 2001, 112). Thus, this common ground could signify a horizontal connection among participants. First, these interviewees referred to themselves and others like them as "halfies," which suggests that there was mutual recognition of a shared likeness or even experience. Second, others viewed mixed-race players as being incomplete or not fully Asian, with one player even being called "White boy" or "White man," first by his coach, and then as a joke by other people. Christie's frustration stems from this lack of complete membership. Root (1997) points out that while being multiracial is complex and varied, there are still "shared phenomenological experiences that make it possible for persons of mixed heritage to assume some bond with one another – and with other multiracial people who do not have Asian ancestry ... and not being counted as a 'real Asian'" is a "common, shared" experience. (31). In light of the literature, the experiences of these four interviewees suggest a connection that operates in relation to and resistance against a vertical axis that emphasizes purity.

Another connection that was based on invented traditions was a sense of shared Asianness or Chineseness, one that existed in parallel with ideas of biological and cultural essentialism, while at the same time contradicting the vertical axis of untainted cultural knowledge as something passed down from one generation to the next. Instead, a sense of shared Asianness or Chineseness was consolidated through learning Chinese from teammates (rather than from parents), through "Asianizing" words, and through the common language of English. As a matter of fact, whereas my inability to understand Chinese languages would have reinforced my outsider position within this study, my lack of linguistic ability rarely proved to be a detriment, in part because Chinese languages were spoken only rarely and almost everyone seemed to be speaking in English. Essentially, by drawing on lateral resources like English, the participants constructed an Asian diaspora that "evokes multiple locations and movements and hesitates to fix itself as a static epistemological object" (Chuh & Shimakawa 2001, 6) and thus does not treat Asianness or Chineseness as being tied to a homeland, essentialized, and homogeneous. This lack of "origins" and a desire for origins are illustrated among the interviewees who make reference to "Asianness" and a sense of identification and belonging as Asians but not to a shared connection to Asia. Furthermore, the reference to multiple locations demonstrates the diversity of Asian diaspora, something that is acknowledged by Nick, for example, who points out that "the Asian make up is a mixed bag of everything," or by other players who do not identify with Chineseness and instead opt to think of the NACIVT and themselves as Asian.

This multiply-located and unfixed Asian diaspora also makes it difficult to describe what Asian diaspora is or the elements upon which belonging in Asian diaspora are based. For the interviewees, their sense of belonging was premised on their relationships with those they deemed to be fellow "Asians" or "Chinese." In general, there was an assumed affinity between Asian people, one that seemed grounded in biological and cultural essentialism (chapter 3). For instance, Nancy explained that two of her close friends are Asian and that "you just feel closer because there's this ... you're both Asian and stuff." Indeed, this presumption is also often called upon in the NACIVT when discussing expansion. A few Canadian interviewees stated that the NACIVT should expand to Vancouver. One long-time player explained that "they tried to get Vancouver involved because of the amount of Asians there, but for some reason, it hasn't worked." Everyone who spoke of expanding to Vancouver based their suggestion on the belief that there were many Asian people in that city. Indeed, Chinese Canadians constitute the largest non-European ethnic group in Canada, with 72 per cent of all Chinese people living in either Toronto or Vancouver (Statistics Canada 2006). However, there is an additional assumption that members of the large Chinese and broader Asian population in Vancouver would inherently wish to play volleyball together.

Asian diasporic belonging was demonstrated in other ways. For example, there is a feeling of shared accomplishment and pride in the size and continuity of the NACIVT. Christie shared her mother's first impression of the tournament. She was

> shocked by it because there were a lot of Asian people and she was really proud of that. My brother came about two years ago, and he brought a couple of his friends, and they were blown away. They were walking around like, "I can't believe there's so many people, all Chin- [cuts herself off] all Asian in one room, I can't believe it."

Similarly, when I first witnessed the tournament that was held in Toronto, I recall feeling awed by the number of Asian people who had attended. I felt moved by their dedication and humbled when I realized that this commitment had helped to maintain the tournament for several decades. In addition, there may also be a sense of dedication or duty to other Asians, as expressed by two interviewees who felt that their respective clubs provided an important service to their community because they helped young people lead a positive lifestyle.

Relationships with other Asians and the identification as Asian *through* these relationships (as opposed to automatic membership) were important for many players and their sense of identity and belonging as Asian. For example, Rob did not grow up in or near a Chinatown and therefore viewed his upbringing as different from that of players who lived in Chinatown and attended high schools that had a large number of Chinese or Asian students. Thus, joining a team that participated in the NACIVT "was in some ways learning about my Asianness." Rob located Asianness within Chinatown, conflating both Chineseness and Asianness in his relationship with other Chinese and Asian people. Another interviewee, Kyle, grew up in a medium-sized city approximately forty-five minutes outside of a large metropolis with a high concentration of Chinese and Asian people. Thus, he explained that there was no Chinese language school for him to attend, that outside of his household he was unaware of other Chinese families, and that his friends were all "Caucasian." Now that he has moved to a bigger city and as a result of his participation in the NACIVT, however, he noted that most of his friends were "Asian" and were involved in the tournament. Indeed, according to Michael, a significant part of the tournament was that it gave "youth of the Chinese or the Asian background a chance to meet." The importance of co-ethnic socializing is also noted in Chin's (2016) study of Japanese American basketball leagues and King-O'Riain's (2006) study on Japanese American beauty pageants.

Similarly, Irene had very few Asian friends when she was growing up and was one of only two Asian students in her school. She recalled with laughter that people would often get the two of them confused. She also remembered playing volleyball against a high school team from a very multicultural city and was "shocked because the whole team was Asian. [...] I was so shocked, I had never seen that before." Now having moved to a diverse urban city[2] and participated in the tournament for a number of years, she notes that her social network has changed dramatically:

> If you looked at pictures that I have from the last two years, two or three years, you wouldn't think I had any non-Asian friends. Because a lot of them happen to be social outings with my volleyball team or like I do go out with certain people from volleyball teams [...] But it looks like I only have Asian friends.

These examples illustrate how the tournament allowed these participants to access an Asian network by forging connections across different communities.

These relationships were especially significant for Erin when she was growing up. As a child, Erin had few Chinese or even Asian friends, and she found this to be especially isolating and lonely. She said that it was a great feeling when she began participating in an NACIVT team and in the tournaments. Her school friends were not familiar with her culture, and because Erin did not speak English well, she faced other challenges such as name-calling and not understanding what was being said. Through the tournament, Erin made Asian friends and felt that she "related better to NACIVT players." There was a sense of identification cultivated through finding similarities, or as she put it, a "feeling that 'Oh, everybody else is like that,' 'All Asian parents raise kids like that.'" This is similar to Kyle's understanding of relationships between him and his Asian friends. Relationships with and relating to other Asian people helped to create a feeling of belonging within Asian diaspora for the participants. As Diane puts it, "The reason you would join something like [the NACIVT] is there's a sense of belonging."

---

2 It should not be presumed that cultivation of diasporic links or transnational ties is not possible in smaller towns. Although Kyle and Irene identified the lack of diversity in their city as a reason for the lack of relationships with other Asians, Chen's (Z. Chen 2004) work illustrates how diasporic phenomena can manifest in small towns and cities.

Related to this sense of connection between Asian people is a feeling of comfort at being among other Asians that is expressed by some interviewees. For Christie, the NACIVT provided "a time to enjoy being Asian and meet other Asians." This sense of comfort was independent of other groups.

Overall, several interviewees indicated that they did seek out connections with other Asian people, and in doing so learned about their "Asianness." When probed, however, a number of respondents had difficulty articulating what this learning entailed, and some even expressed ambivalence about the degree of connection based on "Asianness." One team in particular stands out. This group of players had at one time played together on the same team, were of similar age, had common goals, and had joined the club and begun participating in the tournament at the same time. Thus, they "were a focal point" and bonded over their shared status as being the first second-string team to play in the women's division: "the first idea of the future, that athletes could be better so that the club could get stronger down the road" (member of team). While they no longer play together, the connections and friendships they made are still meaningful, and they socialize with each other regularly. Not once during the interviews with four of the original members did they voluntarily suggest that they felt more comfortable with each other because of a shared sense of culture or heritage. When asked directly about whether Asianness was significant in forging close friendships, one interviewee (identified as "I") hesitated before responding:

Y: What was the significance of being all-Asian? Did being all-Asian matter in your friendships?

I: Probably, I guess. Just 'cause I can more or less relate to them ... in terms of culture, certain things ... like, I don't know, sharing common foods, and uh ... different superstitions that we believe in ... I don't know, just that aspect of it.

It is clear that this player had difficulty articulating her response, pausing numerous times, and was vague and uncertain about the extent to which "Asianness" played a role in creating friendships with her teammates.

Another player, Kyle, was equally ambivalent about the impact of being "fellow Asians" on his relationships with his teammates and other players in the tournament:

> When I talk to people on the circuit, there's a lot more relatable things, just being Asian. I don't know if it's a big difference. My teammates … if you think about it, they all have the same situations as anybody else, like, "I can't make practices," "I have these problems or these issues," or whatever, Asian or not, it would be the same issues.

Kyle at first admits that there is more common ground as a result of being Asian but quickly dismisses its significance, stating that the issues facing players, be they related to or outside of volleyball, are not unique to Asians. Together such comments, along with the multitude of ways in which the participants connected with one another, such as through being teammates or being from the same city or nation (see Nakamura 2016), reinforce Lowe's (1996) argument that the connection among Asian people is not rooted in an unchanging culture or body of knowledge that is passed down from one generation to the next. Clearly, the participants identified other ways through which to bond, and when asked directly about a shared sense of "Asianness," they struggled to articulate how it did or did not influence their connections with one another. Indeed, as the interviews progressed, some unexpected ways in which people bonded through working out their shared "Asian," "Chinese," or other identities became clear, methods that did not *a priori* depend on definitions of who counts as Asian or Chinese.

While interviewees did make reference to a feeling of comfort resulting from the assumption of shared "Asianness," their relationships with their teammates suggest that these connections were not solely based on "Asianness." For example, Diane described how people in her club get to know each other and "some people find out they go to the same school or what not, or they do activities outside of volleyball." Beyond her club, she stated that people develop relationships with other teams during the tournament because

> you see them year-in, year-out. You're competing, you play the same teams. Then you start ... and a lot of times you have time to socialize when you're playing, between games you're reffing, you're cooperating with other teams. [...] and we work with each other, too, especially if you're organizing, too, especially you would know people.

Thus, the relationships within and across teams are built through socializing, competition, recognition of familiar faces, refereeing, collaborating with other teams, and working together. Similarly, Nancy and Karen noted that they developed closer friendships with teammates through commuting to practices together and subsequently using this time to learn more about one another. For a number of interviewees, being part of a team and working towards and achieving goals as a team also helped create a strong bond between players. It is not solely a shared sense of "Asian-ness," then, that creates this community but experiences of connection, collaboration, and cooperation. Simply having a group of Asians together in the same space does not automatically result in intimate relationships. To presume that it would suggests that the relationships between individuals of the same racial or ethnic group are based solely on race or ethnicity. However, these examples, as well as the aforementioned vertical, horizontal, and lateral connections that were cultivated by players, illustrate that human relationships are far more complicated.

Relationships with Chinese people also provided opportunities to learn more about Chineseness in a way that went beyond the vertical axis of passing cultural knowledge from one generation down to the next. For example, Eli, who identified as "half-Chinese," indicated that through his participation he became immersed in Chinese culture, especially as a result of "full Chinese people taking me out and stuff like that, with the older guys and coaches and stuff. I do feel a sense of connection in terms of my Chinese side by playing nine-man." Similarly, Christie felt that her sense of Chineseness was enhanced through "hanging around people who are

Chinese." She felt that the tournament facilitated "learning from people who speak Chinese and people who grew up in a really Chinese household, so I can learn about my own roots and what it's like to be Chinese and stuff, and I appreciate it." Similarly, Lisa indicated that "being associated with the Chinese tournament and being surrounded by a lot more Chinese people has made me *want* to learn more about where my parents come from, where my family, where my *entire* family comes from and what being Chinese really means to me and to other people at least." While there is an emphasis on origins, rather than essentializing Chineseness, Lisa wished to explore the question of what being Chinese means, and recognized that this may vary among different "Chinese" people.

One especially interesting example is how participants bonded through learning to speak Chinese together during their participation in the tournament. While this could be interpreted as the hegemony of Chineseness in the tournament, in the case of one team the fact that a number of players were learning some Chinese words, including when they were used and how they were pronounced, pointed to a horizontal connection among the teammates. One particular player is identified in the tournament as Chinese; however, her immediate roots are not in China, and the trajectories of her family are routed through other locations.[3] Thus, the Chinese dialect that she speaks is not commonly used among players in the circuit. She shared how she and her teammates who do not identify as Chinese learned a few Cantonese words during the course of their participation because their Chinese teammates would speak to each other in this dialect. This player did not feel excluded by their choice of speaking in Chinese. Because of this exposure, she and some teammates picked up a few words. Thus, she observed that "We say '*Aiya*' a lot, like whenever we make a mistake, and certain plays, we'd be like 'tip *jon gan*,' which means like in the middle. We'd be like okay, tip there." She did not use the words she learned from her parents, since they spoke a different dialect from the teammates who were teaching her these words.

---

3 I cannot disclose any further details in order to protect her identity.

Thus, her use of this vocabulary was limited to the volleyball court and to the time spent with her teammates. This interviewee also confessed that "Sometimes it's funny because we're, like, butchering the word, we don't pronounce it properly" or, in other words, are pronouncing it with an English accent. She did not recall other people correcting her pronunciation. Rather, she said that "it's funny because everybody will start speaking Chinese with an English accent." This example illustrates how language is shared along horizontal and lateral axes rather than a vertical one (i.e., parents teaching children how to speak a language). Furthermore, it suggests that horizontal and lateral connections and passing of knowledge outside of the vertical axis may not necessarily be unidirectional or encumbered by notions of purity, and can in fact produce new cultural forms that can still connect people in meaningful ways.

A second related way in which participants were connecting with one another in unexpected ways also involves language. As one interviewee put it:

> We ... I guess, Asianize certain words and, like, talk in a certain accent (laughs) whenever we're around each other. (Female interviewee, former player)

This practice of Asianizing words or speaking English with a Chinese accent was an unexpected lateral connection between players on one particular team. It linked players on her team who were of Chinese descent and who spoke Chinese to those who did not speak Chinese and those who were of non-Chinese Asian backgrounds. A practice that began as a way to make fun of their coach, who "has a really thick Chinese accent, [...] just kinda stayed." The interviewee explained that it was "one of those things we do whenever we see each other, [...] when we get together." I argue that this is a lateral connection because the practice is a result of the players' interaction in English rather than in some common Chinese or other Asian language, and links the players together across difference. Thus, notions of pure culture and restrictive qualifications of identity (Ang 2001) are destabilized. Furthermore, if one takes the view that diaspora can be an alternative sphere, one that is a space of resistance against the push for the purity of the nation (Abdel-Shehid 2005), this act of mimicking how Chinese/Asian people are perceived and mocked in Canada and the United States may be a way to acknowledge and deflect this attempt to reinforce their "lesser-than" status (A. Paz, personal communication, 14 August 2013).[4] The imitating of an Asian accent may also be a type of humour that helps to make this environment more comfortable or is a type of behaviour that is only possible in an Asian space. It is especially telling that the interviewee who recounted this practice noted that it was something she only did with her Asian team-mates and something that was pretty common across the teams that participate in the NACIVT.

Certainly, this practice is not without its problems. While the player who shared this anecdote with me was insistent that other teams that competed in the circuit engaged in the same custom, she was the only one who mentioned it, even when her teammates were interviewed. Nor did I observe other teams engaging in this practice. It is arguably something that, while pleasurable for those who participate, is also tainted by the question of (and perhaps guilt over) whether it is appropriate (a concern that was reflected in the interviewee's laughter as she shared this story), precisely because it belittles Chinese immigrants. Another player from the same club but a different team noted that those players who were born in North America would make fun of players who were born elsewhere. They would "make fun of the accent. It can be done in an endearing or friendly manner. Other times, it really is to make fun of them. This is on an individual basis though ... generally insensitive guys do this." Clearly, an activity that the above inter-viewee identified as something that she does only with her team-mates, that they "all" do, and that has helped to solidify a bond between her and her teammates can also exclude not only those

---

4 Alejandro Paz is an associate professor of anthropology. He is an expert in the role of language in globalization, transnationalism, and diaspora. He has recently published a book on the issue of citizenship in relation to language and language use.

who are being ridiculed but others who see the practice as "insensitive," suggesting that lateral connections can also create divisions. Furthermore, by mocking intonations, it reproduces imperialistic hierarchies whereby certain accents (e.g., British, Canadian, etc.) are valued over accents from other regions (e.g., India, China, etc.).

During another interview, one man who described how he was approached by someone to join a team proceeded to repeat this person's words by imitating what he perceived to be a Chinese accent, laughing afterwards. Because I did not want to jeopardize the rapport that we had established, I was not able to ask why he did this – whether it was because he thought it would be funny or that it was okay because I was a "fellow Asian." Nevertheless, this exchange helps to illustrate further the complexity of this practice of speaking English with a Chinese accent, and to introduce the idea that lateral connections may be contradictory and ambivalent rather than exclusively resistant or transformative in the way that Lowe (1996) describes.

Another way in which difference is reconciled and community is produced is through the primacy of English as the way to connect people who are of different backgrounds. For example, one player noted that language differences were a challenge when he first began to learn how to play nine-man after he immigrated to Canada. He explained that while he is from northern China, most of the players were from a different area and spoke a different dialect. They would have to resort to speaking in English so that he could learn the intricacies of the game. A more recent player stated that "Chinese is not really spoken as much just 'cause there are a lot of CBCs [Canadian-born Chinese] and, uh … I guess there are a lot of people that don't speak Chinese, so the common language is just English" (Amber). These examples illustrate how cultural practices within diaspora are marked by hybridity, in this case by the sharing of cultural knowledge in English and English as the language of communication between people of diverse linguistic backgrounds.

Certainly, Chinese language(s) are ever present in the NACIVT, such as within the tournament booklets or via speeches given during opening ceremonies or during banquet speeches. Furthermore, the ability to speak Chinese, particularly Mandarin, is closely related to Chinese identity (Ang 2001; Tu 1991). The issue of language is especially pertinent, as it is often the marker of Chinese membership and identification (Tu 1991). This was also reinforced by the interviewees. In one instance, for example, when I asked Owen how he identifies himself, he hesitated before responding that he thinks of himself as Chinese Canadian. He immediately started discussing his Chinese speaking ability, how this is limited to communicating with his mother, and how she sometimes has trouble understanding him. His focus on language seems to suggest that his sense of Chineseness is related to the ability to speak a Chinese dialect. Similarly, when I asked Nick whether he thought of himself as Chinese, he began by telling me, "I don't even speak the official language, which is Mandarin. And that is almost like a foreign language to me." He later noted that in Chinatown he did not feel that he was respected because he could not speak the language well but that his volleyball prowess and involvement in NACIVT brought him admiration from the Chinatown community. This example illustrates how hybridity can create new ways of imagining belonging, since Nick felt he was not respected because of his lack of skill in the official language but *was* respected because of his involvement in volleyball. Only after giving this pre-emptive explanation regarding their language (in)ability did these two players identify themselves as Chinese. The ability to speak Chinese was also asserted, in the case of Karen's teammate, as a declaration of her Chinese identity, a statement that was especially important and often necessary, since she was read as half-Chinese. In all three instances, the ability to speak Chinese is hegemonically constructed or equated with authenticity (Ang 2001).

Nevertheless, this link between Chinese identity and Chinese language is still tenuous especially in the NACIVT. Diasporic subjects themselves are marked by cultural, linguistic, and ethnic heterogeneity (Braziel & Mannur 2003), and linguistic difference within the Chinese diaspora is particularly salient within the NACIVT. Nick stated that the issue of identity was complex because most of the early NACIVT participants spoke Toisanese, as they were from the Toisan district. He referred to this language as "a really archaic dialect," one that is rarely spoken among Chinese in the United States and Canada, let alone among current NACIVT participants, thereby implying that this link between language and Chinese identity is dynamic. Furthermore, this Chinese language and its NACIVT connection continues to change because of the increasing number of participants who speak only English. For example, Michael pointed out that a number of fans in his city do not read or speak English and are critical of the lack of Chinese language support:

> They always get on me, "Hey you got to do this, you got to have the Chinese in their uniforms so we could identify who they are and where they're from" because they want to follow [the game]. And I say it's difficult because some of these young teams play six man, and they have their uniform. Are you going to ask them to change uniforms and spend extra money to come over here? So instead I make up a lot of signs on the court, you know. So this year, I already enlist, next year, I already enlist a couple of Chinese writing enthusiasts to write down the rules and how we play, post it on the board, what teams against what in Chinese as well as in English.

This example illustrates how the connection between the NACIVT and Chinese language has changed over time, such that Chinese language is increasingly taking a secondary place behind English as the dominant medium for communication and therefore connection within the NACIVT. It is clear that diasporic subjects are shaped by, in this case, linguistic hybridity, because diaspora does not exist in isolation. Rather, ethnic, cultural, and linguistic diversity occurs in part because the Chinese diaspora exists through interaction with or even at the intersection with other diasporas, including but not limited to the Japanese, Korean, Filipino, and – more broadly – Asian diasporas.

Perhaps the best example of how new traditions and connections are being fostered to reconcile difference and produce community is in the meaning of "Chinatown" within the NACIVT and among its participants. It also illustrates Lowe's (1996) contention that culture is "worked out as much 'horizontally' among communities as it is transmitted 'vertically' in unchanging forms from one generation to the next" (64). The place of Chinatown within the NACIVT reproduces ideas of authenticity and an unchanging homogeneous Chinese culture. It also offers an opportunity for NACIVT participants to reclaim Chinatown not as an ethnic enclave or ghetto but as way to assert "belonging" in the nation and body politic by calling Chinatown home, not only on their own behalf but on that of the Chinese diaspora broadly (see also Nakamura 2012).

Most interviewees associated Chineseness with Chinatown, specifically the Chinatown located in the city's urban core, be it in Toronto or Washington or elsewhere. Furthermore, this Chineseness was intertwined with notions of authenticity. Interviewees often noted that the tournaments began with a parade through Chinatown and that, during the tournament, players would often eat in Chinatown if the site was close by. Lisa described how playing in Chinatown created an atmosphere that could not be reproduced in a convention centre or parking lot:

> It just feels more authentic when it's held on the street and people are hitting balls into buildings and, you know, you have to watch out, you know, breaking windows and having the shopkeepers come out and watch you, but there's no difference in the way that you play the game, but the feel, the atmosphere, it's just, it's that level of authenticity. It's just different to look at your player, to look up and kinda scope out the court and rather than seeing a wall or ... something like that, that you would see inside or, you know, tennis courts, you see, you know, a Chinese restaurant with, you know, barbequed duck in the window (laughs).

Similarly, Nancy stated that there was something different about playing in the streets of Chinatown because of "the smells and stuff like that." These interviewees valued the experience of playing in and around Chinatown – for example, as happens with the New York Mini – and wished to maintain this tradition. Other players, though, preferred indoor, climate-controlled courts because they ensured consistent and optimal playing conditions. For the latter, the experience of the NACIVT had more to do with playing volleyball (another tradition that connected players) than with maintaining the historic practice of playing in Chinatown.

The symbols of Chinatown, such as the Chinese restaurants and shops, the smells, and the image of meat hanging in a shop window, help to provide a sense of "authentic Chineseness" for tournament participants. In addition, Chinese food also added to this experience. Adam, for example, connected "authentic Chineseness" with food, stating that playing in Chinatown provided a sense of "ethnic belonging, let's say. When you're in between games, you can go to a restaurant and get barbequed pork on rice, you can go get some buns, you can get whatever." One organizing committee decided to

> bring in some Chinese chefs from a restaurant and we had them serve Chinese food [...] so teams could go downstairs [...] and they could just buy food there so that was our concession [to hosting the tournament outside of Chinatown], saying let's keep this as authentic as possible.

Eating Chinese food during the tournament is in part tradition – whether that of eating authentic Chinese food or that of a team ritual of eating particular foods during the tournament – and in part convenience. As Rachel puts it, "in between games you can just run across the street and get dumplings for like a dollar." Likewise, Nancy explained that "being in Chinatown, you can order the Chinese food right there." When the tournament was not held in or around Chinatown, participants were observed returning with take-out food from coffee and sandwich shops, hot dog stands, and concession trucks that were close by. On the other hand, one team placed food orders with parents who had come to support their children's team. These parents then went to Chinatown for the requested food, allowing the players to rest between games. This practice was also observed at the Phoenix Cup (in 2015), which takes place in Mississauga and has its own Chinese Centre (www.mississaugachinesecentre.com).

In speaking of Chinatown, most interviewees referred to this place in a routine way, in that this space that they identified as

Chinatown was obvious and needed no explanation. As John and Ava put it, "Chinatown is Chinatown," meaning they were homogeneous, irrespective of location. In the case of New York, Boston, Toronto, San Francisco, and Montreal, however, these cities have more than one Chinatown, each reflecting a number of differences, including migration histories, class, language, level of education, and connection to the NACIVT. In Manhattan and Toronto, the tournament is most closely associated with the Chinatown in the downtown core and not the satellite Chinatowns in Flushing or Brooklyn outside Manhattan and Markham or Mississauga outside Toronto. Similarly, San Francisco and Montreal both have more than one Chinatown. The NACIVT is affiliated with the oldest Chinatowns in these two cities.

A few interviewees acknowledged the impact of having a number of Chinatowns in Toronto and environs, such as the challenge of determining where the tournament should be held. One tournament organizer noted that, if she had had the time, she would have approached the businesses in the other Chinatowns, presuming that since they were "Chinese" and the tournament was "Chinese," they would likely provide financial support. The fact that other Chinatown locations could be considered as potential venues and the speculation that these other Chinatowns would be interested in supporting the tournament suggests that there is a presumed link between Chinatown and the NACIVT, one that is forged through a supposed shared "Chineseness." However, the differences between the Chinatowns are significant. One former player recalled that one year when the tournament was held in Toronto, he "went to the wrong Chinatown. At that time there's two Chinatowns (laughs)." This change in the geographic location of (the NACIVT's) Chinatown signals the division between the various Chinatowns and suggests that they may potentially exist as separate and distinct from each other. Differences in terms of class, language, level of education, relationship to the state, perception by residents and non-residents, location, development, migration histories of residents, and function for Chinese people (e.g., Anderson 1987; Craddock 1999; Kong & Yeoh 2003; Kwong 1996; Lin 1998; Ma 2003; Mercer 1988; Ng 1996; Pan 1990; Pon 2000b;

Waxman n.d.; Zhou & Lin 2005) are not necessarily acknowledged within the NACIVT in its relationship to "Chinatown." This heterogeneity is hidden by the blanket of "authenticity" that all Chinatowns are presumed to have.

The place of "Chinatown" within the minds and experiences of NACIVT players serves as a lateral and horizontal connection, in that it reflects a connection between diasporic nodes rather than between an assumed core or home and away (see also Abdelhady 2006 and Trotz 2006). Further, because of some participants' geographic location, the place of Chinatown becomes defined as the "home" of nine-man specifically and of Chineseness generally. For example, James explained that he grew up in an outlying area of Toronto and consequently had never heard of nine-man volleyball. It was only when he was in university that he was introduced to the sport. However, had he grown up in Chinatown, he explained, it was "automatically understood that you'll be involved in nine-man." Adam reiterated this point, claiming that Asian volleyball players who grew up in the suburbs would have no knowledge of the tournament. Even "A Short History" notes the challenge of geography in accessing Chineseness and the value of the tournament in "bringing young people back into Chinatown from the suburbs [since] Asian youth, growing up in the suburbs are in some ways as isolated as the laundry workers of an earlier generation" (55th Tournament booklet 1999, 26). Through these horizontal relationships (i.e., a shared sense of isolation), the suburbs were interpreted by a number of participants and within the stories repeated in the tournament booklets as a location devoid of Chineseness, while Chinatown was the site of Chinese people and roots. Ironically, in light of the frequent references to Chinese people moving away from Chinatown and into the suburbs, one would think that there are plenty of other Chinese people in the suburbs. Nevertheless, through a horizontal lens, it becomes clear that, for these participants, Chinatown is the "home" to which suburbanites return. In Michael's words, the tournament "brings back the Chinese Americans that have no contact with the Chinese, that move out into the suburbs [...] this is the first time that they have a chance to go back to their roots." Implicit in his comment is the view that the tournaments are for those Chinese who have moved away from the urban core (i.e., Chinatown) and by participating in the NACIVT are returning to their roots (read: Chinatown).

Thus, Chinatown is the location of nine-man volleyball and, more broadly, of Chinese culture in diaspora. James described the players who played for a high school in Chinatown and said "they're obviously more, you know, into the Chinese culture" as a result. Because many Chinese young people no longer live in Chinatown, they are "cut off from their Chinese heritage and the people who make that heritage come alive" (55th Tournament booklet 1999, 26). Thus, participation on the volleyball team was described as "the first chance these young people have to really learn about Chinatown and its culture, and as important [... for meeting] young people from Chinatown" (55th Tournament booklet, 1999, 26). This was reiterated by Adam, who explained,

> You always read about these kids, these Chinese kids, let's say, that are born up in the suburbs, that their only interaction with the Chinese culture is in the summertime playing with their Chinese teammates.

Adam is not clear about where he read or heard these stories, and his account sounds more like an often-repeated narrative based on hearsay. Whether these accounts are true is not important, however. What is important is that he, like others, believes that the tournament provides a conduit for young people who are raised in the suburbs (read: outside of Chinatown) to connect with Chinese people and culture.

The identification with the urban Chinatown may be because these Chinatowns are older or because of the assumption that Chinatown was the point of departure into middle-class suburbia, a place predominantly associated with whiteness. In addition, the lack of connection with suburban Chinatowns may reflect recognition of the diverse ways of being Chinese that are associated with different Chinatowns (Pon 2000b). It may also be indicative of divisions within Chinese communities that are reproduced in the different Chinatowns, as demonstrated by Pon (2000b). One suburban Chinatown in Toronto, for example, is associated with Hong

Kong-born, Cantonese-speaking, more affluent, middle- to upper-middle-class Chinese people who bypassed the downtown Chinatown and arrived in the suburbs directly. Such individuals may deride working-class Canadian-born Chinese as *juk-sing*, mocking their not-quite-Canadian-or-Chinese identities. As individuals living in the suburbs, those players who identified Chineseness as being located in the urban core may do so to avoid and reject the rigid definitions of Chineseness that may be enforced in suburban Chinatowns. Ultimately, the geography of Chineseness that these interviewees delineated reflects the multiple and continually shifting meanings of "Chinatown" and its relationship to Chinese people, as well as the new ways of imagining traditions.

The integrity of a community cannot be maintained entirely by keeping out those who are not welcome. The NACIVT especially, despite the emphasis on notions like tradition, culture, authenticity, and unity in the face of discrimination, is diverse in experiences, geography, age, generation, ethnicity, and a multitude of other dimensions. In the case of Asian immigrants in Western countries, cultural and community continuity are explained along a vertical axis, with an emphasis on the passing down of unchanging values such as respect for elders and on the importance of recognizing generational, age, and structural hierarchies. As Lowe (1996) points out, scholars are also implicated in the repetition of this storyline in their focus on what she calls vertical relationships. Lowe therefore calls for consideration of horizontal relations and the intersection of vertical and horizontal relationships (see, for example, Joo 2012; Thangaraj 2013, 2015a, 2015b; Yep 2009). Taking a broader view enables us to move away from treating culture as an unchanging, static body of knowledge that is passed down from one generation to the next; to critique notions of "authentic" or "pure" culture; and to conceptualize ethnic identity in a more dynamic way, one that is constructed in response to a number of vertical and horizontal relationships.

Relationships that were significant to the participants in this study were both vertical and horizontal/lateral. Vertical relations did not exclusively shape the interviewees' experiences, understanding of culture, or sense of identity. The vertical relationships were also not necessarily confrontational. In fact, they were often significant and meaningful associations, as older players, coaches, alumni, and parents were sources of inspiration, advice, mentoring, support, and tutelage. Although generation gaps were salient and sometimes identified as the reason for conflict, particularly around changes to the rules, interviewees welcomed the presence of older fans, admired players who competed alongside their children, and were eager to continue the legacy of high-level volleyball that had been passed on to them. These relationships are likely not unique to the NACIVT interviewees. Unlike the literature on ethnicity and sports, however, this study points not only to the conflict between immigrant parents and children but also to instances of crossing generation gaps, building bridges across difference, and including people of various generations. It also illustrates how horizontal and lateral relationships shape immigrants' sports experiences.

Consideration of horizontal connections is important because it does not take culture as something that is given and passed down unchanged along a vertical axis. Rather, the (re)production of culture is a much more fluid and negotiated process, one that can occur along horizontal lines and at the intersection of vertical and horizontal connections. Such an approach has implications for a more nuanced understanding of second-generation immigrants and their experiences. For example, in this study, one group of players frequently spoke to one another in English with a Chinese accent, or, when Chinese words were spoken, they would "butcher" the pronunciation. They were engaging in a cultural practice that was possible precisely because they were second-generation immigrants, fluent in English, some less so in Chinese, producing a hybrid cultural knowledge that was shared with friends and peers who were not of the same linguistic background and that resulted in a sense of camaraderie. Juxtaposing this practice with statements from other interviewees who seemed to apologize for not being able to speak Chinese when they claimed their identity as Chinese suggests that identity and culture that are defined along a horizontal axis may be more inclusive than identity and culture that are defined along a vertical one.

Identifying the vertical, lateral, and horizontal relationships and their intersections as they manifest themselves within the NACIVT also illustrates the challenge of understanding the role of the NACIVT in its members' lives. Previous research has found that ethnic sports organizations and tournaments serve multiple functions, such as a medium for assimilation or a way to maintain ethnic ties. The NACIVT does not fit easily into either category. There is evidence of participants' learning citizenship skills, of the growing institutionalization of the sport, and of the loss of nine-man playing styles. Furthermore, the challenges that participants face with regard to intergenerational conflicts are common themes in work that is grounded within an assimilation framework. Nevertheless, the NACIVT does not easily fit into the body of work that shows how sports facilitate assimilation. Even within the vertical relationships identified, for instance, there is a desire to pass on the culture and traditions within the NACIVT. Instead, the NACIVT seems to be more aligned with the scholarship that demonstrates how ethnic identities are maintained, via sports, in response to experiences of racism and discrimination, particularly in light of the origins story of the tournament. However, this too is not an easy categorization because it is not ethnic identity alone that serves as the glue between the various players. A shared passion for volleyball was by far the greatest connector between the participants. Relationships that were unrelated to volleyball were in turn cultivated as a result of shared circumstances, such as being of mixed race. Chinatown facilitated these lateral connections to the extent that it became "home" for the tournament as well as for the participants who otherwise had few or no opportunities to be in Chinatown. Invented "traditions," possible precisely because they were forged across horizontal and lateral connections, illustrate how the community that is constructed through the NACIVT, while racialized, gendered, and classed, also cannot be reduced to these categories. The NACIVT community is actively produced through meaningful connections and traditions fostered by the participants in relation both to difference without and to difference within. And this will be its ongoing challenge.

Photo 4.1 Toronto Flying Tigers and unidentified team, 2013, Washington. The photo shows a right side hit by a Flying Tigers player. The tournament took place on Pennsylvania Avenue. Capitol Hill is visible in the background. Credit: Rosanna U.

Photo 4.2 New York Freemasons and Jin Long, 2018, New York. The photo shows an attack by a left-handed fastball Freemasons player. Two Jin Long players form a block. Credit: Rosanna U.

Chapter 5

Match Point: The Future of the NACIVT

In 2010, at the Boston tournament, a fight broke out during the banquet, the hallmark social event of the Labour Day long weekend. Based on accounts of people who were there and those who heard what happened, it seems that a team from Toronto had acted disrespectfully towards a team from the hosting city. Unfortunately, it was not just *any* Boston team; it was a team that allegedly had affiliations with gangs and a secret society called the Freemasons. One long-time player said that he had always been warned about this particular team and had subsequently cautioned younger teammates to keep their tempers and attitudes in check and "no chirping through the net" when playing against them. It seems this message was not heeded by the Toronto team whose players apparently offended this Boston team.

Footage of the fight, captured in Liang's (2014) documentary film about nine-man, shows plates and chairs being thrown, men posturing and rushing aggressively at others, an elder attempting to calm tempers over the microphone, and other players quickly dispersing from the banquet hall. Police were called to both the banquet site and the hotel where most of the tournament participants were staying. In the film, a young man is seen outside on the street commenting to his friends, "Isn't this supposed to unite Chinese people in America? We're family, man. We're all Chinese people," thumping his chest in a gesture of solidarity. He said it with a small smile, perhaps trying to be light-hearted, but the conflict nevertheless left a sombre mood among the players, as one interviewee described it. She was particularly worried about friends whom she heard had been hurt and threatened. The seriousness of the conflict became all the more real when the team from Toronto was asked to leave and left for Toronto that night. Police remained at the tournament site the following day.

Since then, both teams involved in the altercation continue to participate in the tournament, and not much appears to have changed. It may be that the dominant narrative of celebrating the NACIVT for its solidarity, community, family, and togetherness continues to prevail. Sarah said that she had been told the issue "had been resolved." Boston, however, has not hosted the tournament since. Indeed, 2016 marked what should have been the return of the tournament to Boston, but it was instead held in Los Angeles, with plans to hold the tournament in Orlando in 2017. Beyond this change in tournament site, the impact of the conflict seems to have been minimal; it is treated as an isolated incident and the community is presumed to be stable once more.

Edwards's (2001) work on *décalage*, along with Clifford's (1997) and Brah's (1996) discussions of diaspora, remind us to be suspicious of the stability of community, to see it not as a starting point but as the destination. A seemingly unified, cohesive, utopic collective is produced through stabilizing a former instability (Edwards, 2001). A key task, then, is to identify the strategies through which this occurs. Thus, the focus of this book was to engage with the question of how the collective "we" within the NACIVT is produced; or as Brah (1996) puts it, to consider who is empowered and disempowered, how divisions are negotiated, and the relationship to other collectivities. In this case, the collective "we" is produced primarily through the drawing of boundaries, as well as through passing down supposedly untainted and unchanged cultural knowledge. In other words, through the continuous (re)drawing of boundaries and the line of continuity from a point of origin to the present, the interviewees were simultaneously assuming and constructing a stable, homogeneous, unified community.

I have argued that participation in the NACIVT is important for the interviewees because it provides them with a sense of belonging in a community through the cultivation of relationships with admired players, role models, and older people from whom they can learn about the game, life, and migration experiences. They are able to play a sport they love, strengthen relationships with teammates, make new friends, travel, socialize, and perhaps meet partners. For some, participation is a chance to take part in Chinese culture – such as enjoying the lion dance and multi-course meals at a Chinese restaurant and sharing experiences of growing up as a "Chinese" person; or it provides an opportunity to connect with one's cultural roots. Such descriptions of the meaning of participation in an ethnically and racially exclusive activity may seem superficial, but the importance of being able to feel at home and feel a sense of belonging should not be dismissed. As I grappled with the issue of NACIVT's exclusion of non-Asians, I kept replaying my initial impression of the first tournament I attended. It was an emotional response, a feeling that here I belonged. It was not unlike the sensation I had in the graduate class I took where I had a Chinese professor and one Korean and three Japanese classmates: it was shocking and also wonderful – wonderful that I did not have to explain myself to others. The commitment to maintaining boundaries and interviewees' understanding of their sporting experiences both in and outside of the NACIVT illustrates how racial awareness frames the feeling of belonging and interviewees' participation in the NACIVT and provides the grammar through which their involvement is articulated.

This racial awareness was particularly heightened through a sense interviewees had of being alone and different, both in and outside of sports, and through the burden of the stereotypes they had to overcome, particularly for those interested in playing in mainstream sports, whether volleyball or some other sport. Those who have been selected to play on teams may not be considered as serious opponents (Nakamura, 2004), or may be presumed to be good at only one thing; others may not be selected at all. Stereotypes and the barriers to participating in sports reflect how White racism structures the terrain of understanding difference, such that Whiteness is the norm against which "Asianness" is defined, and "Asian" people are consequently seen to be limited in their abilities. These views may be internalized, or may be expressed in the rationale for imposing boundaries and limits on "half-Asian, half-White" players.

The NACIVT is important because it provides an opportunity to those players who would not otherwise get a chance to play. The significance of the opportunity to learn, hone, and display the sporting prowess of Asians is related to the model-minority myth that frames Asians in Canada and the United States as uninterested in or inept at sports. Asian women are constructed as frail, passive, and docile, and thus presumably unable or too fragile to be participating in sports. Lack of height among Asian men is defined in emasculating and infantilizing ways, and in turn provides a rationale for channelling them either into sports that are less aggressive or out of sports entirely. Being stereotyped as studious (and therefore not athletic) and good at math (and less so at sports) may not seem particularly important. However, when the model-minority myth is contextualized within the relationship between sports, nation, and citizen, the consequences of this stereotyping become clear.

Sports and nation- and citizenship-building are connected to one another in both applied and discursive ways. For example, the vitality of citizens is viewed as an important measurement and reflection of the strength of the nation. Thus, physical education has historically been considered a key element of nation-building (Okay 2003; McNeill et al. 2003). Success at international sporting events, especially the Olympics, is also tied to nation-building in that representatives demonstrate the physical primacy of their nation in a legitimate and universally sanctioned forum. Good citizenship is also thought to be illustrated by health, vitality, strength, and participation in physical activity. With this sports/nation/citizen triad in mind, I suggest that the model-minority myth, which positions Asians as non-sporty, unfit, passive, and timid, serves to reinforce the exclusion of Asians from the nation, equating Asianness with foreignness through an implication that they are "unfit" and therefore not "fit" to be citizens (Nakamura 2012). Together with the exclusion of Chinese men from physical activity spaces that marked the beginning of the NACIVT, the model-minority myth illustrates the role of the sports/nation/citizen triad in the continuity of Asian exclusion from the nation (Nakamura 2012).

It is precisely because of this racial context, a context that defines "Asianness" as foreign and therefore not a mark of citizenship, that the NACIVT is so important and the political stakes of participation in this organization are so high. It is clear that the NACIVT is an alternative cultural realm that illuminates how exclusion from mainstream sports and racialization both within and outside of sports occur. Furthermore, it is an alternative cultural sphere because it is a site where citizenship in terms of skills, characteristics, and physicality can be demonstrated. The NACIVT, with its history and connection to Chinatown, roots Asian people in the nation and acts as a claim of belonging. It is an alternative cultural space because it calls into question narrow and racialized understandings of who is a citizen. And yet, the boundaries of belonging within the NACIVT are problematic because they are highly racialized and restrictive and hierarchize those who are of mixed race. They also rely on and reproduce essentializing views of race, gender, and culture.

The interviewees had differing views about the eligibility rules and the boundaries they enforced. These diverse opinions not only reflect the diversity of the participants themselves but also reveal how identity is socially constructed and is not in fact primordial as the rules seem to suggest. Furthermore, the boundaries that are constructed by the eligibility rules have tangible and emotional consequences. For example, some teams may not continue and may be forced to disband because they are not able to meet the eligibility requirements. Diane recalled a predominantly Korean team that could not field a legal line-up and was forced to break up. The emotional impact of encountering these boundaries should also not be dismissed. Interviewees felt disappointment at not being able to play, despite practising hard and being committed to their team. They felt resigned that there was little they could do, feelings that often led them to end their careers much earlier than their "100 per cent Chinese" counterparts. Interviewees also felt that their place on the team was in flux and uncertain. Even though they were loyal members of their teams, it did not always seem as though they had a stable sense of belonging within the club, with some even suggesting that they did not matter as much as others. Ultimately, many players felt defeated because they came to realize that there was little they could do to change the rules, despite voicing their frustrations and disappointments. Thus, it is arguable that those individuals who felt defeated and resigned were experiencing the hierarchies within and limits of diasporic belonging.

Given their dissatisfaction and the varying and sometimes critical opinions about the eligibility rules, it is no surprise that the future of the eligibility rules is perhaps one of the most pressing issues that the NACIVT is facing. How can unity and continuity be maintained within a context of change and desire for expansion?

In 2014, organizers of a local volleyball tournament in Boston chose to ignore the eligibility rules, allowing anyone to participate in nine-man. It was organized by the Boston Hurricanes Athletic Association, a club established in 1970 to serve the local Asian community via sports programming (Kam 2014). According to Jeff Chin, then president of the Boston Hurricanes volleyball club, the initial impetus for opening up the eligibility rules was because of a shortage of participating teams for an upcoming tournament, a problem that reflected a growing struggle to expand, reignite, and maintain interest in the volleyball club. However, there were also broader changes that were leading to important questions about who belongs, who is a member, and what the NACIVT is intended to promote. Chin describes it as a "strategic conversation" about who is a member of their club, and the subsequent realization that "our kids are not Chinatown-based kids anymore. They are second-generation suburban kids" (Kam 2014, para. 7). Furthermore, the association, and specifically the volleyball club, were realizing that the friendships (or lateral relationships) that young Chinese Americans have are not exclusively Asian (Kam 2014).

Perhaps the most significant change is demonstrated by how Chin redefines culture. When asked whether culture or cultural integrity is jeopardized by opening up the eligibility rules, Chin responds that "Chinese American culture is mixed with Asian American culture. My son's culture is different from my culture" (Kam 2014, para. 11). There is a clear recognition that culture is dynamic, that significant lateral connections are forming, and that culture is being produced at these points of interaction (Clifford 1997). Interestingly, Chin does not appear to grieve generational differences, which is in stark contrast to the vertical approach or treating culture as unchanging. Instead, Chin defines anew the culture of the NACIVT as the practice of connecting, sharing, and playing together across difference (Kam 2014). This view was reiterated by other interviewees as well (Helen, Luke, Ava).

Ignoring the eligibility rules was possible because this tournament was a local event. Even Chin admitted that "we took some liberties because we could" (Kam 2014, para. 16). But Boston is not alone. A number of people at the Phoenix Cup (Toronto 2015) mentioned that the rules are not enforced at local Toronto tournaments. Chin, too, noted that organizers in Washington had been rethinking the rules (Kam 2014). These grassroots changes may be the start of a growing movement to reconsider who can play, one that may, in turn, shift ideas about how community is produced and stabilized.

Conversations about belonging and who is "Chinese" and/or "Asian" must take place alongside a shift in how "Chineseness" and/or "Asianness" are constructed and what is imagined as possible for Asian people in the sporting realm and beyond. But this is no easy task. There is internal pressure to maintain rigid terms of membership in response to outside pressures like discrimination and racist imagery, external forces that remain salient and may seem more immediate than broader claims of the fluidity of identity. In our discussion of opening up nine-man to non-Asian players, one alumnus showed me a photo that had been circulating among his NACIVT friends. It was a picture of a team that had won a local Chicago nine-man tournament in the summer of 2015. They were a team of all White men called "White on Rice." As he showed it to me, the man shook his head and said, "It's so bad." He then proceeded to show me one of the comments posted in response that called it the "Thief Team" and that said, "Soon they will come for our women and our spices like Marco Polo." The team name "White on Rice" is quite unlike the name "Polar Bears" adopted by a predominantly White team that played in the tournament organized by the Boston Hurricanes. The former reproduces the stereotypical connection between "Asianness" and rice and figuratively alludes to White domination of Asians. Whiteness is made visible through disparaging Asianness. This participant showed me the picture and comment to illustrate the risk in opening up the tournament entirely – a complex reaction, focusing on the risk of being stereotyped and of having something that is "theirs" being taken and exploited, expressed by a commentator speaking from a position of victimhood but at the same time reducing women to chattel.

To intervene in the racialized social construction of Asianness necessitates recognition of the ever-present reality of race and racism and how they structure not just our everyday lives but our sporting experiences. At present, this intervention into the social construction of Asian athleticism remains triangulated with and against Whiteness primarily and Blackness generally. As Chin described it, "They'll look at us differently. They'll see that these guys are pretty good and that's not a bad thing to have" (Kam 2014, para. 13; see also Liang 2014). While I do not wish to dismiss the significance of having successful Asian American/Canadian volleyball players as role models, the status of the invisible "they" remains unchanged, and the racial landscape of Asian-/White-/Black-ness also stays unquestioned. Just as Jeremy Lin, an Asian American professional basketball player who shot to fame in 2012, astutely questioned why his skills were consistently described as "deceptive" (as cited in Wang 2015), we must be alert and attuned to when and how Asianness is considered "different" and in relation to what norm(s)? Who is making the claim or labelling Asians as "unlikely" or "unexpected" athletes? These are important questions to ask because they make visible how race and racism structure our desire for successful Asian athletes.

What lies ahead for the future of the NACIVT? Over a decade ago when I first started studying the NACIVT, Lisa said that the presence of mixed-race players and the eligibility rules would be *the* issue that members would have to address in the coming years. This statement may still be true, and how to proceed may still be very contentious. In Liang's (2014) film, Reggie Wong, a highly respected elder from Boston, shares a joke he used to say to his children: "Your mom and I are 100 per cent Chinese. Who's going to screw it up? (laughs)." I acknowledge that Wong may have meant this entirely in jest. However, the desire to maintain the purity of the NACIVT is still a subtext in his words, especially when taken together with the idea of passing on something that is "diluted" and the subsequent need to maintain boundaries (NACIVT participants' comments featured in Liang 2014). One older player admitted to me that he and his wife are proud that their child is "100 per cent" Chinese, though he acknowledged that "a lot of our close friends, they're mixed couples." And yet because of their own inability to speak a Chinese language fluently, it was clear that they felt that the "authentic" Chineseness of their child was questionable.

Mixed-race players and the eligibility rules are "a problem" because of another change related to the increasingly competitive tournaments and players' desire to win. Teams are recruiting top players, and players are switching teams so that they may increase their chances of being on a championship team. By contrast, in the past, "It was all about loyalty, it was all about family, you know you play with that one team you stick with that one team and that's it. And now it's like we're like trading cards" (Phoebe). In fact, a different concern that I noticed over the past decade is the critique of the increasing number of intercollegiate and elite-level players who are recruited as a "ringer" for a team and do not necessarily commit to practices throughout the season leading up to the Majors. The "traditions" that the eligibility rules are intended to protect are changing by the increasing emphasis on winning. The sense of camaraderie, the relationships and connections that are fostered through shared experiences of practices and working hard – the very things that the players a decade ago claimed were protected in part by the eligibility rules – are becoming increasingly devalued. Furthermore, with the recruitment of highly skilled sixes players, much of the nine-man style of play has been lost or discarded. Such moves are considered "inefficient," as Luke, a long-time student of volleyball and of nine-man observed: "If the team wants to be really competitive – the good teams, you'll see, they never do any nine-man moves [...] Very seldom do they do that." In other words, the "authenticity" of nine-man is disappearing.

The anxiety over losing authenticity, particularly in an age of mass reproduction, is discussed by V.J. Cheng (2004) in his work on Irishness. He poses the question of whether mechanically reproduced authenticity is then still authentic? Within such a quandary, Cheng states that there is a focus on the past and on origins in order to justify the present. Though the circumstances affecting the elements of nine-man are quite different from those affecting the Irishness that Cheng examines, the paradox of authenticity has parallels here, with the variation of examining what is authentic nine-man volleyball in an age of the institutionalization of sport? Just as mass reproduction results in sameness and consistency (and therefore loss of distinctiveness), institutionalized sport ensures uniformity and reliability in terms of rules, officiating, and even tournament site. These were elements that were lauded by the participants, while the authentic elements of nine-man were being discarded in favour of sixes volleyball technique. As these aspects of authentic nine-man become devalued, the "authentic" may become increasingly symbolized by the bodies of "authentic" Chinese and Asian people, bringing us back to the "dilemma" of mixed-race individuals.

There are a number of factors in play here. Racism and discrimination operate to stereotype Asian people and limit their opportunities in and outside of sports. The ongoing exclusion of Others from playing volleyball within the NACIVT is justified by this external pressure but is also framed by narrow ideas of race as biological and culture as innate, and of women as marginal within the sporting realm. There are also internal pressures to maintain the authenticity of the event and the community, which further justify the eligibility rules. Nonetheless, external pressures such as changing demographics and even more expansive understandings of "Asia," together with voices of resistance from within the NACIVT, particularly around mixed-race players, are calling the exclusion of Others into question. There are two competing realities of race in the NACIVT, with different risks and consequences for each. One views "race" as real in terms both of biology and of its discriminatory effects; the other sees "race" as socially constructed and therefore not a solid foundation upon which to build community. Both approaches require individuals, groups, and communities to face the challenge of how to deal with difference.

Lisa is in part correct. Mixed-race players and the eligibility rules continue to be a critical issue that the NACIVT community must address. The eligibility rules focus entirely on race/ethnicity/ nation and are grounded in socially constructed commonalities rooted in biological essentialism. The future of the NACIVT hinges on a broader and deeper discussion of what the NACIVT is now, who it is for, and what will bind its diverse members together in an ever-changing context. Within a globalized context where information is exchanged at lightning speed and the course of change can shift at the whim of social media, what is the future of the NACIVT and how will it reconcile community-building goals with more inclusive and dynamic terms of membership? Chin described the NACIVT culture as something new, produced through playing and connecting with others (Kam 2014). The evidence would suggest that the NACIVT community has always been produced in relation to difference – different cities, nations, and languages. This lack of unity, homogeneity, and consistency over time can be jarring. For if we do not have a common origin and shared cultural elements and if Asianness or Chineseness as a "race" is a social construction, then we are left with nothing (V.J. Cheng, 2004). The solution is not to recuperate the stability of this category but to view community as in process and, thus, authenticity as not possible. While this can be destabilizing and can certainly reduce political clout (see Espiritu 1992), by bringing its production to the forefront, we can avoid buying into essentializing narratives and make room for difference, allowing for diverse historical and cultural circumstances as well as for invented traditions and change. Perhaps the NACIVT community needs to tell different versions of its histories, so that it may direct its future.

Appendix: Methods and Procedures

This study of the NACIVT is a multi-sited ethnography that entails in-depth interviewing, participant-observation, and textual analyses. The study was conducted with approval from the University of Toronto research ethics board and following institutional ethical research guidelines.

In-Depth Interviewing

The primary method used was in-depth interviewing, following a semi-structured interview guide.

Interview Guide

Demographic Data: Name, age, occupation, place of birth [duration in Canada or the United States], language spoken; when people ask "what are you?" what do you say?

- What roles have you played in the NACIVT (e.g., player, coach, organizer, sponsor, fan, etc.)?
- What teams have you played for in the NACIVT?

Participation in Nine-Man Volleyball (for male interviewees)

- How did you come to start playing nine-man volleyball?

- How is playing with just Chinese or Asians different from other teams you've been on?

Nines vs Sixes (for female interviewees)

- Tell me the about the status of 6s versus 9s in NACIVT.

Participation in North American Chinese Volleyball

- Tell me about the most memorable tournament you participated in. [Where was it? Who did you go with? What are your fondest memories of the first tournament? Did you win? Who did you meet?]
- Was the tournament in Chinatown? What is the difference between playing and not playing in or close to Chinatown? Does it matter whether it's in Chinatown?
- Tell me about the tournaments in the different host cities.
- What do you look forward to as Labour Day approaches?
- Tell me what happens during pool play when you're not playing. Who do you cheer for? What about when it's Canadian vs US teams?
- Tell me about social events that take place during the tournament?
- Voluntary activities relating to the team:

  - What are they?
  - What are the challenges of fundraising?
  - If some people don't participate in the fundraising, what happens? How are these individuals perceived?

- What other volleyball opportunities are you, your teammates, your club involved in? Are they Asian- or Chinese-only tournaments/leagues?
- Tell me about the friendship tourney to China – what do you know about it? Did you go? Why or why not? What did the trip mean to you, your family, your teammates?

Relationships with Others

- What kind of challenges are there within your team? with your coach?

- What role do your teammates have in your life, off the court? What about the people you meet at the tournament?

Expectations as a Volleyball Player

- What expectations do you have to meet as a member of your team/club?
- Tell me about any conflicts you've seen or heard on your team? [How was it resolved?]
- Do you see any differences in how the men's team and women's team is expected to behave?

Rules re: Eligibility

- Tell me your views regarding the eligibility rules.
- What do you think is the rationale for this rule?
- Whose responsibility is it to make sure the other team is abiding by this rule?
- Tell me about any conflicts that you saw or heard about regarding this rule?
- What do you think is the future of this rule?
- What would happen if the tournament became totally open to all Asians? To everybody?
- As a coach ...

    – What challenges does this rule pose for you as a coach?

Organizing Committee

- Tell me the specific details of what the tournament organizing committee is responsible for.
- What kind of sponsors do you approach and why?
- What kinds of challenges arise when trying to organize a tournament?
- What made you want to help organize the tournament? Would you do it again?
- Did you have any relationships with the Chinese business community (like the CCBA [Chinese Consolidated Benevolent

Association] in the US)? Tell me about the relationship between the organizing committee and this community? What are the advantages and challenges in working with this association? What is their role? What influence does the CCBA have in how the tournament operates, in the rules, in decision making?

The NACIVT in General

- What changes have you seen over the course of your participation?
- What is the significance of the NACIVT to the Asian or Chinese community? To the volleyball community?
- The NACIVT has continued for over 60 years – what does it mean for you to be a part of that history?
- What keeps you going back to the tournaments?
- What hopes do you have for the future of the tournament?

Recruitment Strategies

- Through known contacts
- Through snowball sampling

Interviewees

- Targeted individuals: different teams, genders, levels of involvement (coach, alumni, captain, player, elder, tournament organizer, organizing committee chair, and so on), cities, age groups, ethnoracial identification

Participant Observation – Observer as Participant

Tournaments Observed

- Toronto, Ontario, on 3–5 September 2005
    - Press conference held one week prior to the tournament
    - Opening ceremonies
    - Awards ceremony

- Washington, DC, on 2–4 September 2006

    - Observations initiated on 1 September 2006
    - Included Captain's Meeting

- New York Mini, New York City, New York, on 22–3 July 2006
- Phoenix Cup, Mississauga, Ontario, on 15 August 2015

Practices Observed

- 1 Toronto team (Summer 2015)

Strategies for Observation

- "Easy openings" (Glesne 1999, 47)
- Noting the setting, participants, events, acts within events, and people's gestures (Glesne 1999)
- Broad sweep and trying to record everything, observing nothing in particular in order to see what stands out, looking for paradoxes, and lastly, any problems facing the participants being observed (Wolcott 1981, as cited by Glesne 1999)

Textual Analysis

In addition to the interview and participant-observation data, textual data were analysed.

Websites

The following is a list of websites analysed in this project. Many of these websites are no longer active, or have changed in design and content during the last ten years.

The North American Chinese Invitational Volleyball Tournament Website

www.nacivt.com

This website was active until approximately December 2006, after which time it appears the domain name expired and subsequent visits to the site would result in a new page that was unrelated to the tournament. On 1 December 2007, a new website was launched under this domain name that subsequently leads visitors to an updated website URL for an upcoming tournament or provides information for an upcoming tournament.

New York Mini

www.nymini.com

Until 2007, the nymini.com website included information on the history of the New York Mini, as well as other information such as the Friendship Tourney to China. However, the website was temporarily shut down for reasons unknown. When the website was relaunched, much of this information was no longer on the website and the site was dedicated only to information about the upcoming mini tournaments.

NACIVT – Toronto, Canada, 2005

http://www.realkool.com/nacivt/index.html

This website is no longer active.

NACIVT – Washington, DC, 2006

http://www.dcnacivt.com/index.htm

This website is no longer active. A new website was launched – www .dc.nacivt.com – for the 2013 tournament.

NACIVT – San Francisco, CA, 2007

http://www.nacivt-sf.com

This website became temporarily unavailable in March 2008 and has been inaccessible ever since.

Captain's Meeting (2006) – documents

- 2006 DC NACIVT Protest Process
- Captain's Meeting PowerPoint Slides
- Schedule and Tournament Information, Women's Division, 62nd North American Chinese Invitational Volleyball Tournament
- Schedule and Tournament Information, Men's Division, 62nd North American Chinese Invitational Volleyball Tournament

Tournament Booklets

I examined eight tournament booklets from 1999 to 2003 and 2005 to 2007. Tournament booklets are often coveted by the players, and organizers frequently run out of copies by the end of the first day. In 2014, the booklet was available online through the tournament website.

The booklets are listed below.

55th Tournament booklet. (1999). *Boston 1999 55th Annual North American Chinese Invitational Volleyball Tournament*. Boston.

56th Tournament booklet. (2000). *56th Annual North American Chinese Invitational Volleyball Tournament*. Toronto.

57th Tournament booklet. (2001). *57th Annual North American Chinese Invitational Volleyball Tournament*. Washington, DC.

58th Tournament booklet. (2002). *58th Annual North American Chinese Invitational Volleyball Tournament*. San Francisco.

59th Tournament booklet. (2003). *Annual North American Chinese Invitational Volleyball Tournament*, 30 August–1 September, New York.

61st Annual North American Chinese Invitational Volleyball Tournament. (2005). Retrieved 21 August 2005, from www.realkool.com/nacivt /index.htm.

62nd Annual North American Chinese Invitational Volleyball Tournament. (2006). Washington, DC. Retrieved from www.dcnacivt.com/index.htm.

63rd Annual North American Chinese Invitational Volleyball Tournament. (2007). San Francisco. Retrieved 19 July 2007, from www.nacivt-sf.com/.

72nd Annual North American Chinese Invitational Volleyball Tournament. (2016). LA NACIVT Team Roster and Waiver Form. Retrieved 4 August 2016 from http://www.nacivtla.com/#!registration/c24vq.

Strategies for Textual Analysis

- Informal analysis (Peräkylä 2005)
- For example, noting the types of letters of support, advertising, photos, and languages that were used in the booklet and recurring themes across the different tournament websites, paying particular attention to movement, how community was constructed or assumed to be given, and the place or erasure of difference.

Strategies for Analysis

- Inductive and deductive coding
- Resource: LeCompte & Schensul 1999
- Kvale (1996): to ask explicit questions of the data. In this study, questions inspired by my subjective feelings – intrigue, confusion, surprise, and curiosity – whereby I served "as both recorder and filter" (Borkan 1999, p. 181)
- Systematic approach to coding as outlined by LeCompte and Schensul (1999)

Rigour

Accuracy and believability were achieved by using open-ended questions, by interviewing a number of people of various positions within the tournament, and by asking questions in different ways. Transparency was achieved through making it clear and obvious the questions that guided the analysis of the interview transcripts, such that the process of interpretation is apparent. A related strategy is the practice of reflexivity, where I considered the various positions I occupied throughout the course of the study, and their implications for my interpretations, reactions, subjectivities, and analyses.

The following is a list of sources that influenced and guided my research methodology, procedures, and analysis:

Acker, S. (2000). In/out/side: Positioning the researcher in feminist qualitative research. *Resources for Feminist Research, 28*(1/2), 189–208.

Clifford, J., & Marcus, G. (Eds). (1986). *Writing culture: The poetics and politics of ethnography*. Berkeley, CA: University of California Press.

Denzin, N.K. (1970). *The Research Act in sociology*. Chicago: Aldine.

Denzin, N.K., & Lincoln, Y. (Eds). (2005). *Handbook of qualitative research* (3rd ed.). Thousand Oaks, CA: Sage.

Glesne, C. (1999). *Becoming qualitative researchers: An introduction* (2nd ed.). New York: Addison Wesley Longman.

Guba, E.G., & Lincoln, Y.S. (2005). Paradigmatic controversies, contradictions, and emerging confluences. In N.K. Denzin & Y.S. Lincoln (Eds), *Handbook of qualitative research* (2nd ed., 191–216). Thousand Oaks, CA: Sage.

Hammersley, M., & Atkinson, P. (1995). *Ethnography: Principles in practice* (2nd ed.). London: Routledge.

Haraway, D. (1998). Situated knowledges: The science question in feminism and the privilege of partial perspective. *Feminist Studies, 14*(3), 575–97.

hooks, b. (1990). Culture to culture: Ethnography and cultural studies as critical intervention. In: *Yearning: Race, gender, and cultural politics* (123–33). Boston, MA: South End Press.

Islam, N. (2000). Research as an act of betrayal: Researching race in an Asian community in Los Angeles. In F.W. Twine & J. Warren (Eds), *Racing research, researching race: Methodological dilemmas in critical race studies* (35–66). New York: New York University Press.

Khan, S. (2001). Performing the native interviewee: Doing ethnography from the margins. *Canadian Journal of Women and the Law, 13*(2), 266–84.

Kvale, S. (1996). *InterViews: An introduction to qualitative research interviewing*. Thousand Oaks, CA: Sage Publications.

Lather, P. (1991). *Getting smart: Feminist research and pedagogy with/in the postmodern*. New York: Routledge.

LeCompte, M.D., & Schensul, J.J. (1999). Analyzing and interpreting ethnographic data. In *Book 5 of ethnographer's toolkit*. Walnut Creek, CA: AltaMira Press.

Marcus, G.E. (1995). Ethnography in/of the world system: The emergence of multi-sited ethnography. *Annual Review of Anthropology, 24*, 95–117.

Naples, N.A. (2003). *Feminism and method: Ethnography, discourse, and activist research*. London: Routledge.

Peräkylä, A. (2005). Analyzing talk and text. In N.K. Denzin & Y.S. Lincoln (Eds), *Handbook of qualitative research* (2nd ed., 869–86). Thousand Oaks, CA: Sage.

Rubin, H.J., & Rubin, I.S. (2004). *Qualitative interviewing: The art of hearing data* (2nd ed.). Thousand Oaks, CA: Sage.

Smith, L.T. (1999). *Decolonizing methodologies: Research and Indigenous peoples.* New York: Zed Books.

Thomas, J. (1993). *Doing critical ethnography.* Newbury Park, CA: Sage.

Young, Jr, A.A. (2004). Experiences in ethnographic interviewing about race: The inside and outside of it. In M. Bulmer & J. Solomos (Eds), *Researching race and racism* (187–202). London: Routledge.

References

Abdelhady, D. (2006). Beyond home/host networks: Forms of solidarity among Lebanese immigrants in a global era. *Identities: Global Studies in Culture and Power, 13*(3), 427–53.

Abdel-Shehid, G. (2005). *Who da man? Black masculinities and sporting cultures.* Toronto: Canadian Scholar's Press.

Agergaard, S., & Ryba, T.V. (2014). Migration and career transitions in professional sports: Transnational athletic careers in a psychological and sociological perspective. *Sociology of Sport Journal, 31*(2), 228–47.

American Volleyball Coaches Association. (2015, December). *Volleyball fast facts.* Retrieved from https://www.avca.org/res/uploads/media/VOLLEYBALL-FAST-FACTS-12-15-.pdf.

Anderson, K.J. (1987). The idea of Chinatown: The power of place and institutional practice in the making of a racial category. *Annals of the Association of American Geographers, 77*(4), 580–98.

Ang, I. (2001). *On not speaking Chinese: Living between Asia and the West.* London: Routledge.

Anthias, F. (1998). Evaluating "diaspora": Beyond ethnicity. *Sociology, 32*(3), 557–81.

Birrell, S., & Theberge, N. (1994). Ideological control of women in sport. In D.M. Costa & S.R. Guthrie (Eds), *Women and sport: Interdisciplinary perspectives* (341– 59). Champaign, IL: Human Kinetics.

Borkan, J. (1999). Immersion/crystallization. In B.F. Crabtree & W.L. Miller (Eds), *Doing qualitative research* (2nd ed., 179–94). Thousand Oaks, CA: Sage.

Bourdieu, P. (1978). Sport and social class. *Social Science Information, 17*(6), 819–40.

Brah, A. (1996). *Cartographies of diaspora: Contesting identities*. London: Routledge.

Braziel, J.E., & Mannur, A. (2003). *Theorizing diaspora: A reader*. Malden, MA: Blackwell Publishers.

Brubaker, R. (2005). The "diaspora" diaspora. *Ethnic and Racial Studies, 28*(1), 1–19.

Bruhn, J.G. (2005). *The sociology of community connections*. New York: Springer.

Canada's Dairy Farmers & CAAWS. (2016). *Women in sport: Fueling a lifetime of participation: A report on the status of female sport participation in Canada*. Retrieved from http://www.caaws.ca/e/wp-content/uploads/2016/03/FWC_ResearchPublication_EN_7March2016.pdf.

Canadian Heritage. (2013). *Sport participation 2010 research paper*. Retrieved from http://publications.gc.ca/collections/collection_2013/pc-ch/CH24-1-2012-eng.pdf.

Carrington, B. (1998). Sport, masculinity, and black cultural resistance. *Journal of Sport & Social Issues, 22*(3), 275–98.

Carrington, B. (2002). Fear of a black athlete: Masculinity, politics and the body. *New Formations, 45*, 91–110.

CCNC (Chinese Canadian National Council). (n.d.). *Chinese Canadian National Council Toronto chapter – history*. Retrieved from http://www.ccnctoronto.ca/about-us/history/.

Chen, A.S. (1999). Lives at the center of the periphery, lives at the periphery of the center: Chinese American masculinities and bargaining with hegemony. *Gender and Society, 13*(5), 584–607.

Chen, Z. (2004). Building the Chinese diaspora across Canada: Chinese diasporic discourse and the case of Peterborough, Ontario. *Diaspora, 13*(2), 185–210.

Cheng, C.I. (2013). Asian American firsts. In *Citizens of Asian America: Democracy and race during the Cold War* (85–115). New York: New York University Press.

Cheng, V.J. (2004). *Inauthentic: The anxiety over culture and identity*. New Brunswick, NJ: Rutgers University Press.

Chin, C.B. (2012). *Hoops, history and crossing over: Boundary making and community building in Japanese American youth basketball leagues*. Unpublished doctoral dissertation, University of California, Los Angeles, CA.

Chin, C.B. (2016). "We've got team spirit!": Ethnic community building and Japanese American youth basketball leagues. *Ethnic and Racial Studies, 39*(6), 1070–88. doi:10.1080/01419870.2015.2203878.

Choi, P.Y.L. (2000). *Femininity and the physically active woman*. London: Routledge.

Chou, R.S., & Feagin, J.R. (2015). *Myth of the model minority: Asian Americans facing racism*. New York: Routledge.

Christian, M. (2011). Mixing up the game: Social and historical contours of black mixed heritage players in British football. In D. Burdsey (Ed.), *Race, ethnicity and football: Persisting debates and emergent issues* (131–44). London: Routledge.

Chronological highlights. (n.d). Retrieved from https://www.fivb.org /TheGame/ChronologicalHighlights.htm.

Chuh, K. (2003). *Imagine otherwise: On Asian Americanist critique*. Durham, NC: Duke University Press.

Chuh, K., & Shimakawa, K. (Eds). (2001). *Orientations: Mapping studies in the Asian diaspora*. Durham, NC: Duke University Press.

Chun, G.H. (2000). *Of orphans and warriors: Inventing Chinese American culture and identity*. New Brunswick, NJ: Rutgers University Press.

Classics game. (2007). Retrieved 11 August 2007, from www.nacivt-sf.com /classic_game.htm.

Clifford, J. (1997). *Routes: Travel and translation in the late twentieth century*. Cambridge, MA: Harvard University Press.

Craddock, S. (1999). Embodying place: Pathologizing Chinese and Chinatown in nineteenth-century San Francisco. *Antipode, 31*(4), 351–71.

Dagbovie, S.A. (2007). Star-light, star-bright, star damn near white: Mixed-race superstars. *Journal of Popular Culture, 40*(2), 217–37.

de Finney, S. (2010). "We just don't know each other": Racialised girls negotiate mediated multiculturalism in a less diverse Canadian city. *Journal of Intercultural Studies, 31*(5), 471–87.

Djao, W. (2003). *Being Chinese: Voices from the diaspora*. Tucson, AZ: University of Arizona Press.

Edwards, B.H. (2001). The uses of diaspora. *Social Text, 19*(1), 45–73.

Elueze, R., & Jones, R.L. (1998). A quest for equality: A gender comparison of the BBC's TV coverage of the 1995 World Athletics Championships. *Women in Sport and Physical Activity Journal, 7*(1), 45–67.

Eng, D., & Hom, A. (Eds). (1998). *Q & A: Queer in Asian America*. Philadelphia, PA: Temple University.

Espiritu, Y.L. (1992). *Asian American panethnicity: Bridging institutions and identities*. Philadelphia, PA: Temple University Press.

Fleras, A. (2011). *Unequal relations: An introduction to race, ethnic, and Aboriginal dynamics in Canada*. Toronto: Pearson Canada.

Fong, E., & Ooka, E. (2006). Patterns of participation in informal social activities among Chinese immigrants in Toronto. *The International Migration Review, 40*(2), 348–74.

Fong, E., & Wilkes, R. (2003). Racial and ethnic residential patterns in Canada. *Sociological Forum, 18*(4), 577–602.

Fung, R. (1996). Looking for my penis: The eroticized Asian in gay video porn. In R. Leong (Ed.), *Asian American sexualities: Dimensions of the gay and lesbian experience* (37–49). New York: Routledge.

Gems, G.R. (1999). Sports, war and ideological imperialism. *Peace Review, 11*(4), 573–6.

Glesne, C. (1999). *Becoming qualitative researchers: An introduction* (2nd ed.). New York: Addison Wesley Longman.

Goosen, T. (1992). *Jin Guo: Voices of Chinese Canadian women*. Toronto: Women's Press.

Gupta, A., & Ferguson, J. (1992). Beyond culture: Space, identity, and the politics of difference. *Cultural Anthropology, 1*, 6–23.

Hafiz, Y. (2013, 16 September). Nina Davuluri's Miss America 2014 win prompts Twitter backlash against Indians, Muslims. *The Huffington Post*. Retrieved from http://www.huffingtonpost.ca/entry /nina-davuluri-miss-america-religion_n_3934428.

Halbert, C., & Latimer, M. (1994). Battling gendered language: An analysis of the language used by sports commentators in a televised co-ed tennis tournament. *Sociology of Sport Journal, 11*(3), 309–29.

Hall, M.A. (1996). *Feminism and sporting bodies*. Champaign, IL: Human Kinetics.

Hess, R. (2000). "Ladies are specially invited": Women in the culture of Australian Rules Football. *International Journal of the History of Sport, 17*(2), 111–41.

Holmlund, C.A. (1994). Visible difference and flex appeal: The body, sex, sexuality, and race in the *Pumping Iron* films. In S. Birrell & C.L. Cole (Eds), *Women, sport, and culture* (299–313). Champaign, IL: Human Kinetics.

Howell, C.D. (1995). The "Others": Race, ethnicity, and community baseball. In *Northern sandlots: A social history of Maritime baseball* (171–95). Toronto: University of Toronto Press.

Humber, W. (1995). *Diamonds of the north: A concise history of baseball in Canada*. Toronto: Oxford University Press.

Hune, S. (2002). Demographics and diversity of Asian American college students. *New Directions for Student Services, 97*, 11–20.

James, C.E. (2005). *Race in play: Understanding the sociocultural worlds of student athletes*. Toronto: Between the Lines.

johnson, j., & Holman, M.J. (Eds). (2004). *Making the team: Inside the world of sports initiations and hazing*. Toronto: Canadian Scholar's Press.

Joo, R.M. (2012). *Transnational sport: Gender, media and global Korea*. Durham, NC: Duke University Press.

Kam, K. (2014, 4 July). *Spiking tradition*. Open City: Asian American Writers' Workshop. Retrieved from http://opencitymag.com/spiking-tradition.

Kibria, N. (1998). The contested meanings of "Asian American": Racial dilemmas in the contemporary US. *Ethnic and Racial Studies, 21*(5), 939–58.

Kim, C.J. (1999). The racial triangulation of Asian Americans. *Politics & Society, 27*, 105–38. doi:10.1177/0032329299027001005.

King, C.R. (Ed.). (2015). *Asian American athletes in sport and society*. New York: Routledge.

King-O'Riain, R.C. (2002). "Eligible" to be Japanese American: Multiraciality in basketball leagues and beauty pageants. In L.T. Võ & R. Bonus (Eds), *Contemporary Asian American communities: Intersections and divergences* (120–33). Philadelphia, PA: Temple University.

King-O'Riain, R.C. (2006). *Pure beauty: Judging race in Japanese American beauty pageants*. Minneapolis, MN: University of Minnesota Press.

Kong, K., & Yeoh, B. (2003). Nation, ethnicity, and identity: Singapore and the dynamics and discourses of Chinese migration. In L.J.C. Ma & C. Cartier (Eds), *The Chinese diaspora: Space, place, mobility and identity* (193–219). Lanham, MD: Rowman & Littlefield Publishers Inc.

Kumashiro, K.K. (1999). Supplementing normalcy and otherness: Queer Asian American men reflect on stereotypes, identity, and oppression. *Qualitative Studies in Education, 12*(5), 491–508.

Kwong, P. (1996). *The new Chinatown*. New York: Hill & Wang.

Laurendeau, J., & Sharara, N. (2008). "Women could be every bit as good as guys": Reproductive and resistant agency in two "action" sports. *Journal of Sport and Social Issues, 32*(1), 24–47.

Lee, C. (2003). *Prostitutes and picture brides: Chinese and Japanese immigration, settlement, and American nation-building, 1870–1920*. Working Paper, Centre for Comparative Immigration Studies, University of California, San Diego, CA. Retrieved 25 November 2005, from www.ccis-ucsd.org /publications/wrkg70.pdf.

Lee, K. (2013). SARS and its resonating impact on the Asian communities. *Leheigh Review, 21*, Paper 24. Retrieved from http://preserve.lehigh.edu /cas-lehighreview-vol-21/24.

Lee, S. (2003). Model minorities and perpetual foreigners. In M. Sadowski (Ed.), *Adolescents at school: Perspectives on youth, identity and education* (41–9). Cambridge, MA: Harvard University Press.

Lee, S.M., & Boyd, M. (2007). Marrying out: Comparing the marital and social integration of Asians in the US and Canada. *Social Science Research, 37*, 311–29.

Lee, Y. (2005). A new voice: Korean American women in sport. *International Review for the Sociology of Sport, 40*(4), 481–95.

Lee, Y. (2015). Beyond black and white: Chinese American women's experiences in sports. In C.R. King (Ed.), *Asian American athletes in sport and society* (13–31). New York: Routledge.

Lei, J.L. (2003). (Un)necessary toughness? Those "loud black girls" and those "quiet Asian boys." *Anthropology & Education Quarterly, 34*(2), 158–81.

Leung, C., & Guan, J. (2004). *Yellow peril revisited: Impact of SARS on the Chinese and Southeast Asian Canadian communities.* Toronto: The Chinese Canadian National Council.

Lew, N. (2007). *Aging greatness.* Retrieved 18 June 2007, from www.nacivt-sf .com/aging_greatness_pt1.htm.

Lew, R. (2007). My heritage. Retrieved 11 June 2007, from www.nacivt-sf .com/my_heritage.htm.

Li, P.S. (1994). Unneighbourly houses or unwelcome Chinese: The social construction of race in the battle over "monster homes" in Vancouver. *International Journal of Comparative Race and Ethnic Studies, 1*, 47–66.

Li, P.S. (2003a). Initial earnings and catch-up capacity of immigrants. *Canadian Public Policy, 29*(3), 319–37.

Li, P.S. (2003b). The place of immigrants: The politics of difference in territorial and social space. *Canadian Ethnic Studies, 35*(2), 1–13.

Liang, U. (Producer & Director). (2014). *9-man.* San Francisco, CA: Center for Asian American Media.

Lin, J. (1998). *Reconstructing Chinatown: Ethnic enclave, global change.* Minneapolis, MN: University of Minnesota Press.

Lowe, L. (1996). *Immigrant acts: On Asian American cultural politics.* Durham, NC: Duke University Press.

Ma, L.J.C. (2003). Space, place and transnationalism in the Chinese diaspora. In L.J.C. Ma & C. Cartier (Eds), *The Chinese diaspora: Space, place, mobility and identity* (1–49). Lanham, MD: Rowman & Littlefield Publishers Inc.

Maclear, K. (1994). The myth of the "model minority": Re-thinking the education of Asian Canadians. *Our Schools, Our Selves, 5*(3), 54–76.

Maeda, D.J. (2012). *Rethinking the Asian American Movement.* New York: Routledge.

Magee, W., Fong, E., & Wilkes, M. (2007). Neighbourhood ethnic concentration and discrimination. *Journal of Social Policy, 37*(1), 37–61.

Mayeda, D.T. (1991). From model minority to economic threat. *Journal of Sport and Social Issues, 23*, 203–17.

McGehee, R.V. (1997). Volleyball: The Latin American connection. *International Council for Health, Physical Education, Recreation, Sport and Dance, 33*(4), 31–5.

McNeill, M., Sproule, J., & Horton, P. (2003). The changing face of sport and physical education in post-colonial Singapore. *Sport, Education and Society, 8*(1), 35–56.

Mengel, L.M. (2001). Triples – the social evolution of a multiracial panethnicity: An Asian American perspective. In D. Parker & M. Song (Eds), *Rethinking mixed race* (99–116). London: Pluto Press.

Mercer, J. (1988). New faces on the block: Asian Canadians. *The Canadian Geographer, 32*(4), 360–2.

Messner, M.A. (1988). Sports and male domination: The female athlete as contested ideological terrain. *Sociology of Sport Journal, 5*, 197–211.

Messner, M.A. (2002). *Taking the field: Women, men and sports.* Minneapolis, MN: University of Minnesota Press.

Millington, B., Vertinsky, P., Boyle, E., & Wilson, B. (2008). Making Chinese-Canadian masculinities in Vancouver's physical education curriculum. *Sport, Education and Society, 13*(2), 195–214.

Mitchell, K. (2004). *Crossing the neoliberal line: Pacific Rim migration and the metropolis.* Philadelphia, PA: Temple University Press.

Morris, A. (2000). "To make the four hundred million move": The late Qing Dynasty origins of modern Chinese sport and physical culture. *Comparative Study of Society and History, 42*(4), 876–906.

Mukharji, P.B. (2008). "Feeble Bengalis" and "big Africans": African players in Bengali football club. *Soccer and Society, 9*, 273–85.

NACIVT.com guestbook. (n.d.). Retrieved 19 November, 2004, from www.nacivt.com/book.htm.

NACIVT-SF (nacivt-sf.com Forum). (n.d.). *And in conclusion of the 63rd Annual NACIVT tournament*. Retrieved from nacivt-sf.com on 8 September 2007.

Nakamura, Y. (2004). *Finding a way, finding the self: The journeys of nine physical education students pursuing "non-traditional" paths.* Unpublished Master's Thesis, Faculty of Physical Education and Health, University of Toronto, Toronto.

Nakamura, Y. (2009). Understanding the challenges of pursuing physical activity. *Physical and Health Education Journal, 75*(2), 18–23.

Nakamura, Y. (2012). Playing in Chinatown: A critical discussion of the nation/sport/citizen triad. In J. Joseph, S. Darnell, & Y. Nakamura (Eds), *Race and sport in Canada: Intersecting inequalities* (213–36). Toronto: Canadian Scholar's Press, Inc.

Nakamura, Y. (2016). Rethinking identity politics: The multiple attachments of an "exclusive" sport organization. *Sociology of Sport Journal, 33*, 146–55. doi:10.1123/ssj.2015-0062.

Nakashima, C.L. (2005). Asian American studies through (somewhat) Asian eyes: Integrating "mixed race" into the Asian American discourse. In K. Ono (Ed.), *Asian American studies after critical mass* (111–20). Malden, MA: Blackwell Publishers.

National Federation of State High School Associations (NFHS). (2014–15). *2014–15 High school athletics participation survey.* Retrieved from http://www.nfhs.org/ParticipationStatics/PDF/2014-15_Participation_Survey_Results.pdf.

Newsweek. (1971). Success story: Outwhiting the whites. *21*, 24–5.

New York Mini. (2006). Retrieved 31 May 2006, from www.nymini.com.

New York Times. (1970, 13 December). Orientals find bias is down sharply in US. *1*, 70.

Ng, W.C. (1996). Challenging an immigrant discourse: The rise of local-born Chinese in Vancouver, 1945–1970. *Journal of American-East Asian Relations, 5*(2), 113–34.

Okamoto, D.G. (2006). Institutional panethnicity: Boundary formation in Asian-American organizing. *Social Forces, 85*(1), 1–25.

Okay, C. (2003). Sport and nation building: Gymnastics and sport in the Ottoman State and the Committee of Union and Progress, 1908–18. *International Journal of the History of Sport, 20*(1), 152–6.

Ong, A. (1998). Flexible citizenship among Chinese cosmopolitans. In P. Cheah & B. Robbins (Eds), *Cosmopolitics: Thinking and feeling beyond the nation* (134–62). Minneapolis, MN: University of Minnesota Press.

Ong, A. (1999). *Flexible citizenship: The cultural logics of transnationality.* Durham, NC: Duke University Press.

Ono, K. (2008). Retracing an intellectual course in Asian American Studies. In *A companion to Asian American studies* (1–14). Oxford: Blackwell Publishing.

Ontario Volleyball Association. (2015). *Annual report 2015.* Retrieved from https://www.ontariovolleyball.org/sites/default/files/2015%20Annual%20Report%20-%20FlipBook.pdf.

Pan, L. (1990). *Sons of the Yellow Emperor: The story of the overseas Chinese.* London: Secker & Warburg.

Park, H. (2007). Constituting "Asian women": Canadian gendered orientalism and multicultural nationalism in an age of "Asia Rising." Unpublished doctoral thesis, Ontario Institute for Studies in Education of the University of Toronto, Toronto.

Peräkylä, A. (2005). Analyzing talk and text. In N.K. Denzin & Y.S. Lincoln (Eds), *Handbook of qualitative research* (2nd ed., 869–86). Thousand Oaks, CA: Sage.

Pew Research Center. (2012). Chapter 1: Portrait of Asian Americans. In *Rise of Asian Americans.* Retrieved from http://www.pewsocialtrends.org/2012/06/19/chapter-1-portrait-of-asian-americans/.

Pew Research Center. (2017). *Chinese in the US fact sheet.* Retrieved from http://www.pewsocialtrends.org/fact-sheet/asian-americans-chinese-in-the-u-s/.

Pirinen, R.M. (1997). The construction of women's positions in sport: A textual analysis of articles on female athletes in Finnish women's magazines. *Sociology of Sport Journal, 14*(3), 283–301.

Pon, G. (2000a). The art of war of the wedding banquet? Asian Canadians, masculinity and antiracism education. *Canadian Journal of Education, 25*(2), 139–51.

Pon, G. (2000b). Beamers, cells, malls and Cantopop: Thinking through the geographies of Chineseness. In C. James (Ed.), *Experiencing difference* (222–34). Halifax: Fernwood Publishing.

Pronger, B. (1992). *The arena of masculinity: Sports, homosexuality and the meaning of sex.* Toronto: University of Toronto Press.

Putney, C. (2001). *Muscular Christianity: Manhood and sports in protestant America, 1880–1920.* Cambridge, MA: Harvard University Press.

Razack, S., & Fellows, M.L. (1998). The race to innocence: Confronting hierarchical relations among women. *Journal of Gender, Race and Justice, 1*(2), 335–52.

Regalado, S.O. (1992). Sport and community in California's Japanese American "Yamato Colony," 1930–1945. *Journal of Sport History, 19*(2), 130–43.

Regalado, S.O. (2000). Incarcerated sport: Nisei women's softball and athletics during Japanese American internment. *Journal of Sport History, 27*(3), 431–44.

Reitz, J.G. (2001a). Immigrant success in the knowledge economy: Institutional change and the immigrant experience in Canada, 1970–1995. *Journal of Social Issues, 57*(3), 579–613.

Reitz, J.G. (2001b). Immigrant skill utilization in the Canadian labour market: Implications of human capital research. *Journal of International Migration and Integration, 2*(3), 347–78.

Romero, J.E. (1985). History of LEFA. *Polyphony, 7*(1), 29–30.

Root, M.P.P. (1997). Multiracial Asians: Models of ethnic identity. *Amerasia Journal, 23*(1), 29–41.

Root, M.P.P. (2002). A Bill of Rights for racially mixed people. In P. Essed & D.T. Goldberg (Eds), *Race critical theories: Text and context* (355–68). Malden, MA: Blackwell Publishers Inc.

Rules and eligibility. (2007). Retrieved from http://www.nacivtla.com /#!blank-2/ic03r.

Safran, W. (1991). Diaspora in modern societies: Myths of homeland and return. *Diaspora, 1*(1), 83–99.

Saito, N.T. (1997). Model minority, yellow peril: Functions of "foreignness" in the construction of Asian American legal identity. *Asian Law Journal, 4*, 71–95.

Sakamoto, I., & Zhou, Y.R. (2005). Gendered nostalgia: Experiences of new Chinese skilled immigrants in Canada. In V. Agnew (Ed.), *Diaspora, memory and identity: A search for home* (209–29). Toronto: University of Toronto Press.

Salaff, J., Greve, A., & Xu, L. (2002). Paths into the economy: Structural barriers and the job hunt for skilled PRC migrants in Canada. *International Journal of Human Resource Management, 13*(3), 450–64.

Schultz, J. (2005). Reading the Catsuit: Serena Williams and the production of Blackness at the 2002 US Open. *Journal of Sport and Social Issues, 29*(3), 338–57.

A short history of volleyball in Chinatown and the Annual North American Chinese Invitational Volleyball Tournament. (1999). *Boston 1999 55th Annual North American Chinese Invitational Volleyball Tournament* (21–7). Boston, MA.

Spickard, P. (2001). The subject is mixed race: The boom in biracial biography. In D. Parker & M. Song (Eds), *Rethinking mixed race* (76–98). London: Pluto Press.

Sports, culture, history, 9-man volleyball in DC. (2006). Retrieved from www.dcnacivt.com.

Statistics Canada. (2006). *The Chinese community in Canada.* Retrieved from www.statcan.gc.ca/pub/89-621-x/89-621-x2006001-eng.htm.

Sugiman, P. (2004). Memories of internment: Narrating Japanese Canadian women's life stories. *Canadian Journal of Sociology, 29*(3), 359–88.

Takaki, R. (1989). *Strangers from a different shore: A history of Asian Americans.* New York: Penguin.

Thangaraj, S. (2013). Competing masculinities: South Asian American identity formation in Asian American basketball leagues. *South Asian Popular Culture, 11*(3), 243–55.

Thangaraj, S. (2015a). *Desi hoop dreams: Pickup basketball and the making of Asian American masculinity.* New York: New York University.

Thangaraj, S. (2015b). "Liting it up": Indo-Pak basketball and finding the American-ness in South Asian American institutions. In C.R. King (Ed.), *Asian American athletes in sport and society* (47–66). New York: Routledge.

Theberge, N. (1994). Toward a feminist alternative to sport as a male preserve. In S. Birrell & C. Cole (Eds), *Women, sport and culture* (181–92). Champaign, IL: Human Kinetics.

Trotz, D.A. (2006). Rethinking Caribbean transnational connections: Conceptual itineraries. *Global Networks, 6*(1), 41–59.

Tu, W. (Ed.). (1991). *The living tree: The changing meaning of being Chinese today.* Stanford, CA: Stanford University Press.

USA Volleyball. (2007). *Demographics* [PowerPoint slides]. Retrieved from http://www.teamusa.org/USA-Volleyball/About-Us/~/media/E20F954B3AD449C48F3970B1E9BA6C33.ashx.

Voigt-Graft, C. (2004). Towards a geography of transnational spaces: Indian transnational communities in Australia. *Global Networks, 4*(1), 25–49.

Volleyball Canada Development Model. (n.d.). *High school.* Retrieved from www.vcdm.org/athletes/resources/high-school.

"Volleyball story." (n.d). Retrieved from http://www.fivb.org/en/volleyball/History.asp.

Walseth, K. (2006). Sport and belonging. *International Review for the Sociology of Sport, 41*(3/4), 447–64.

Wang, A. (2000). Asian and White boys' competing discourses about masculinity: Implications for secondary education. *Canadian Journal of Education, 25*(2), 113–25.

Wang, O. (2015). Living with Linsanity: A retro-diary of the Jeremy Lin phenomenon. In C.R. King (Ed.), *Asian American athletes in sport and society* (172–88). New York: Routledge.

Waxman, S. (n.d.). *The history of New York's Chinatown.* Retrieved 5 July 2008, from http://www.ny.com/articles/chinatown.html.

White, P., & McTeer, W. (1990). Sport as a component of cultural capital: Survey findings on the impact of participation in different types of sport on educational attainment in Ontario schools. *Physical Education Review, 13*(1), 66–71.

Willms, N. (2010). *Japanese-American basketball: Constructing gender, ethnicity, and community.* Unpublished doctoral dissertation, University of Southern California, Los Angeles, CA.

Women rules and regulations. (n.d.). Retrieved from http://www.nacivtla .com/#!blank-2/ic03r.

Wong, J. (1999). Asian women in sport. *Journal of Physical Education, Recreation & Dance, 70*(4), 42–3.

Wu, E.D. (2013). Introduction: Imperatives of Asian American citizenship. In *The color of success: Asian Americans and the origins of the model minority* (1–9). Princeton, NJ: Princeton University Press.

Yep, K. (2009). *Outside the paint: When basketball ruled at the Chinese playground.* Philadelphia, PA: Temple University Press.

Yu, H. (2002). Tiger Woods at the center of history: Looking back at the twentieth century through the lenses of race, sports, and mass consumption. Adapted from an essay in M. Williard & J. Bloom (Eds), *Sports matters: Race, recreation, and culture.* New York: New York University Press. Retrieved from https://www.history.ubc.ca/documents/faculty /yu/Tiger_Woods_Center.pdf.

Zhou, M., & Lin, M. (2005). Community transformation and the formation of ethnic capital: Immigrant Chinese communities in the United States. *Journal of Chinese Overseas, 1,* 2, 260–84.

Index

Photos, figures, and tables are indicated by page numbers in italics.

Lightning Source UK Ltd.
Milton Keynes UK
UKHW011009101219
355098UK00011B/240/P